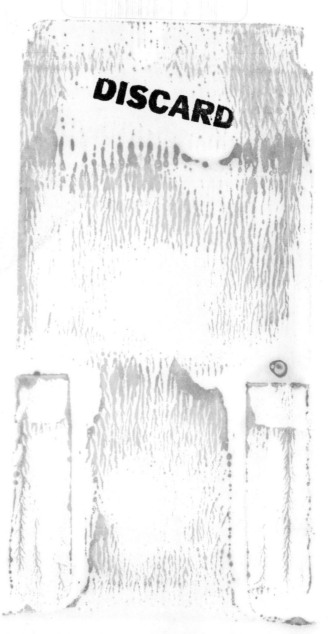

MYTH AND METHOD

Myth and
Method

Modern Theories of Fiction

Edited by

James E. Miller, Jr.

A Bison Book Original
University of Nebraska Press
1960

Copyright © 1960 by the University of Nebraska Press.
Library of Congress catalog card number 60-12941.
Manufactured in the United States of America.

Published September, 1960
Second printing, July, 1961
Third printing, November, 1963
Fourth printing, June, 1965
Fifth printing, October, 1969

Preface

The New Criticism of fiction shares much with its counterpart in poetry. Both came into being as a violent reaction to the heavy-handed, often irrelevant, frequently superficial criticism which was relentlessly historical, biographical, and "moral." In the process of development, both came to place an overriding emphasis on an examination of the formalistic elements of art—in poetry on the explication of the text, in fiction on the analysis of technique. And, finally, in both there has begun a search for greater profundity and deeper meaning, not by a return to the old-fashioned moralistic view, but in an increasingly complex and comprehensive quest for myth and archetype.

The nine essays gathered together in this volume have been selected to suggest that the groundwork for this revolution in the criticism of fiction was laid as far back as the late nineteenth century; that the revolution early gained momentum and carried the day in the twentieth; and that currently, in mid-century, the revolutionary forces are being consolidated while radical, new campaigns are planned.

The several essays have been grouped to suggest this thematic and historical development in the criticism of fiction. The essays under "Artists and Theories" suggest that it was the artists themselves who launched the rebellion and provided the basic revolutionary documents. The essays on "Craft and Technique" indicate that it was the critical and academic mind that formulated and codified the theory for the New Criticism of fiction. And the essays of "Openings and Extensions" imply that it is both the artist and the critic, fretting under the rigidity of the new doctrines, who have ventured forth into unexplored territory, and who, significantly, have discovered a critical meeting-ground for fiction and poetry.

Much, of course, has been omitted and simplified to make this basic direction of fictional criticism clear. Indeed, one of the hindrances in identifying the New Criticism of fiction has been an embarrassment of riches. It is easy for the modern reader to become absorbed into the staggering amount of fiction itself, or to become lost in the accumulated criticism of individual writers, or to become hopelessly entangled in bewildering works promoting isolated theories.

For these reasons the selection has been severe. These nine essays, however, not only illustrate the central movement of fictional criticism in our time: they also are basic critical documents, embodying general principles, offering seminal ideas, advancing fundamental theories—all of immense provocative value for the student, the critic, the novelist, even for the ordinary reader of fiction who wants to benefit from the insights of some of the finest, most venturesome of our critical minds.

If any essay may lay claim to being the basic revolutionary document, surely it is Henry James' "The Art of Fiction." And like all such documents it is primarily an attack on prevailing views, particularly on a debased critical vocabulary that placed a premium on such vague terms as "romance," "novel of incident," "novel of character," and "story." As long ago as 1884, James was pleading for the critic to grant the novelist his subject and to direct attention to his art. And in examining a series of reigning critical clichés, he questioned the insistence on a "conscious moral purpose" by suggesting that the novelist's only purpose (like the painter's) should be to create as perfect a work as possible: "The deepest quality of a work of art will always be the quality of the mind of the producer." In Joseph Conrad's 1897 Preface to *The Nigger of the 'Narcissus,'* we sense the presence of one of those deep-delving minds that inevitably render a work profound, here brooding over the central problems of craft ("to make you hear, to make you feel . . . to make you *see*") as well as over the ever-elusive but perpetually tantalizing "glimpse of truth." In "Notes on Writing a Novel" (about fifty years later), Elizabeth Bowen attempts a cryptic synthesis of the principles of craft that is Aristotelian in its analytical breadth—and also, indeed, in its assertion of the transcendence of action over character. But echoing here and there in the essay, and coming to haunt it like an amnesic term in search of identity, is her phrase, "poetic truth."

If James' "Art of Fiction" was the ringing manifesto, Percy Lubbock's *The Craft of Fiction* (1921) was the new constitution of the revolutionary party, codifying the wisdom of the master—particularly James' Prefaces to his New York edition of 1907-1909. Lubbock's treatment of "Point of View" is almost as logical and tidy as a mathematician's discussion of an equation, surprisingly lacking in the traditional blurred edges and fuzzy conclusions of fictional criticism. His simple but sweeping claim: the "whole intricate question of method" may be resolved into a question of the point of view. In Robert Humphrey's *Stream of Consciousness in the Modern Novel* (1954), a psychologist's term, taken over by the New Criticism to describe a complex fictional technique, is elevated to the level of genre—a new kind of novel of psychological drama. Thus a novel's technique becomes its subject matter as well, and determines its basic category. An indication of this central role of technique was foreshadowed in Mark Schorer's "Technique as Discovery" (1948): "Everything is technique which is not the lump of experience itself." Schorer's main contribution is to demonstrate the close relationship of style and point of view to "thematic definition." Technique seems finally to contain within itself the key to meaning as well as to literary judgment.

Clearly such extravagant claims for technique could not pass without challenge. Such a challenge was made as long ago as 1927, in E. M. Forster's deceptively simple *Aspects of the Novel*. In "Pattern and Rhythm," after an extended and illuminating analysis of the pattern of one of James' novels, Forster declares against its intellectually imposed neatness, and asserts his preference for the less studied and more haunting, intuitive, and organic *rhythm* of Proust's big, sprawling work. Fiction, says Forster, must not seek "completion," a tidy "rounding off," but must discover the "expansion," the "opening out" of music.

In *Quest for Myth* (1949), Richard Chase suggests the possible sources for the deeper rhythms of fiction—a way of expansion and opening out. In defining myth as literature, in accepting it as "a narrative resurrection of a primeval reality," and in asserting that myth dramatizes the fundamental psychological clash between the ego and the objective world, with the alternating attempts of the one to "coerce" the other (in primitive societies, the clash between magic and religion)—with these radical, new approaches Chase proposes fresh ways of discovering and discussing the old profundities of art.

And Northrop Frye, in "The Archetypes of Literature," attempts a comprehensive synthesis of critical views that is breathtaking in its scope. He declares that the conflicting "schools" of criticism are not mutually exclusive but simply represent different critical perspectives on a work of literature. Up close the literary critic is naturally involved in structural analysis (as the art critic is with the brush work), but as he steps back he begins to see other significant elements and relationships until he reaches the limits of perspective, from which he sees the archetypal patterns that connect with other works and that go back to "pre-literary categories such as ritual, myth and folk tale."

In these last essays fictional criticism seems on the verge of both a conclusion and a beginning. The period of uncertainty and doubt, which led frequently to overstatement and dogma, is drawing to a close; ahead lie the possibilities of a comprehensive synthesis, of broader vision and deeper insight. The inexhaustible works of art, the classic novels of old and new, may now yield more of their secrets than ever before. They may now reveal not only their complex craft and technique, their intricate patterns and submerged rhythms. They may also reveal their veiled sources of vitality, their buried roots reaching down in the individual to the deepest springs of being, and stretching back in time to the earliest springs of the human spirit.

JAMES E. MILLER, JR.

Contents

I ARTISTS AND THEORIES

1

The Art of Fiction

BY HENRY JAMES

I should not have affixed so comprehensive a title to these few remarks, necessarily wanting in any completeness upon a subject the full consideration of which would carry us far, did I not seem to discover a pretext for my temerity in the interesting pamphlet lately published under this name by Mr. Walter Besant. Mr. Besant's lecture at the Royal Institution—the original form of his pamphlet—appears to indicate that many persons are interested in the art of fiction, and are not indifferent to such remarks, as those who practise it may attempt to make about it. I am therefore anxious not to lose the benefit of this favourable association, and to edge in a few words under cover of the attention which Mr. Besant is sure to have excited. There is something very encouraging in his having put into form certain of his ideas on the mystery of story-telling.

It is a proof of life and curiosity—curiosity on the part of the brotherhood of novelists as well as on the part of their readers. Only a short time ago it might have been supposed that the English novel was not what the French call *discutable*. It had no air of having a theory, a conviction, a consciousness of itself behind it—of being the expression of an artistic faith, the result of choice and comparison. I do not say it was necessarily the worse for that: it would take much more courage than I possess to intimate that the form of the novel as Dickens and Thackeray (for instance) saw it had any taint of incompleteness. It was, however, *naïf* (if I may help myself out with another French word); and evidently if it be destined to suffer in any way for having lost its *naïveté* it has now an idea of making sure of the corresponding advantages. During the period I have alluded to there was a comfortable, good-humoured feeling abroad that a novel is a novel, as a pudding is a pudding, and that our only business with it could be to swallow it. But within a year or two, for some reason or other, there have been signs of returning animation—the era of discussion would appear to have been to a certain extent opened. Art lives upon discussion, upon experiment, upon curiosity, upon variety of attempt, upon the exchange of views and the comparison of standpoints; and there is a presumption that those times when no one has anything particular to say about it, and has no reason to give for practice or preference, though they may be times of honour, are not times of development—are times, possibly even, a little of dulness. The successful application of any art is a delightful spectacle, but the theory too is interesting; and though there is a great deal of the latter without the former I suspect there has never been a genuine success that has not had a latent core of conviction. Discussion, suggestion, formulation, these things are fertilizing when they are frank and sincere. Mr. Besant has set an excellent example in saying what he thinks, for his part, about the way in which fiction should be written, as well as about the way in which it should be published; for his view of the 'art,' carried on into an appendix, covers that too. Other labourers in the same field will doubtless take up the argument, they will give it the light of their experience, and the effect will surely be to make our interest in the novel a little more what it had for some time threatened to fail to be—a serious, active, inquiring interest, under protection of which this delightful study may, in moments of confidence, venture to say a little more what it thinks of itself.

It must take itself seriously for the public to take it so. The old superstition about fiction being 'wicked' has doubtless died out in England; but the spirit of it lingers in a certain oblique regard directed toward any story which does not more or less admit that it is only a joke. Even the most jocular novel feels in some degree the weight of the proscription that was formerly directed against literary levity: the jocularity does not always succeed in passing for orthodoxy. It is still expected, though perhaps people are ashamed to say it, that a production which is after all only a 'make-believe' (for what else is a 'story'?) shall be in some degree apologetic—shall renounce the pretension of attempting really to represent life. This, of course, any sensible, wide-awake story declines to do, for it quickly perceives that the tolerance granted to it on such a condition is only an attempt to stifle it disguised in the form of generosity. The old evangelical hostility to the novel, which was as explicit as it was narrow, and which regarded it as little less favourable to our immortal part than a stage-play, was in reality far less insulting. The only reason for the existence of a novel is that it does attempt to represent life. When it relinquishes this attempt, the same attempt that we see on the canvas of the painter, it will have arrived at a very strange pass. It is not expected of the picture that it will make itself humble in order to be forgiven; and the analogy between the art of the painter and the art of the novelist is, so far as I am able to see, complete. Their inspiration is the same, their process (allowing for the different quality of the vehicle) is the same, their success is the same. They may learn from each other, they may explain and sustain each other. Their cause is the same, and the honour of one is the honour of another. The Mahometans think a picture an unholy thing, but it is a long time since any Christian did, and it is therefore the more odd that in the Christian mind the traces (dissimulated though they may be) of a suspicion of the sister art should linger to this day. The only effectual way to lay it to rest is to emphasize the analogy to which I just alluded—to insist on the fact that as the picture is reality, so the novel is history. That is the only general description (which does it justice) that we may give of the novel. But history also is allowed to represent life; it is not, any more than painting, expected to apologize. The subject-matter of fiction is stored up likewise in documents and records, and if it will not give itself away, as they say in California, it must speak with assurance, with the tone of the historian. Certain accomplished novelists have a habit of giving themselves away which must often bring tears to the eyes of people who take their fiction seriously. I was lately struck, in reading over many pages of Anthony Trollope, with his want of discretion in this particular. In a digression, a parenthesis or an aside, he concedes to the reader that he and this trusting friend are only 'making believe.' He admits that the events he narrates have not really happened, and that he can give his narrative any turn the reader may like best. Such a betrayal of a sacred office seems to me, I confess, a terrible crime; it is what I mean by the attitude of apology, and it shocks me every whit as much in Trollope as it would have shocked me in Gibbon or Macaulay. It implies that the novelist is less occupied in looking for the truth (the truth, of course I mean, that he assumes, the premises that we must grant him, whatever they may be) than the historian, and in doing so it deprives him at a stroke of all his standing-room. To represent and illustrate the past, the actions of men, is the task of either writer, and the only difference that I can see is, in proportion as he succeeds, to the honour of the novelist, consisting as it does in his having more difficulty in collecting his evidence, which is so far from being purely literary. It seems to me to give him a great character, the fact that he has at once so much in common with the philosopher and the painter; this double analogy is a magnificent heritage.

It is of all this evidently that Mr. Besant is full when he insists upon the fact that fiction is one of the *fine* arts, deserving in its turn of all the honours and emoluments that have hitherto been reserved for the successful profession of music, poetry, painting, architecture. It is impossible to insist too much on so important a truth, and the place that Mr. Besant demands for the work of the novelist may be represented, a trifle less abstractly, by saying that he demands not only that it shall be reputed artistic, but that it shall be reputed very artistic indeed. It is excellent that he should have struck this note, for his doing so indicates that there was need of it, that his proposition may be to many people a novelty. One rubs one's eyes at the thought; but the rest of Mr. Besant's essay confirms the revelation. I suspect in truth that it would be possible to confirm it still further, and that one would not be far wrong in saying that in addition to the people to whom it has never occurred that a novel ought to be artistic, there are a great many others who, if this principle were urged upon them, would be filled with an indefinable mistrust. They would find it difficult to explain their repugnance, but it would operate strongly to put them on their guard. 'Art,' in our Protestant communities, where so many things have got so strangely twisted about, is supposed in certain circles to have some vaguely injurious effect upon those who make it an important consideration, who let it weigh in the balance. It is assumed to be opposed in some mysterious manner to morality, to amusement, to instruction. When it is embodied in the work of the painter (the sculptor is another affair!) you know what it is: it stands there before you, in the honesty of pink and green and a gilt frame; you can see the worst of it at a glance, and you can be on your guard. But when it is introduced into literature it becomes more insidious—there is danger of its hurting you before you know it. Literature should be either instructive or amusing, and there is in many minds an impression that these artistic preoccupations, the search for form, contribute to neither end, interfere indeed with both. They are too frivolous to be edifying, and too serious to be diverting; and they are moreover priggish and paradoxical and superfluous. That, I think, represents the manner in which the latent thought of many people who read novels as an exercise in skipping would explain itself if it were to become articulate. They would argue, of course, that a novel ought to be 'good,' but they would interpret this term in a fashion of their own, which indeed would vary considerably from one critic to another. One would say that being good means representing virtuous and aspiring characters, placed in prominent positions; another would say that it depends on a 'happy ending,' on a distribution at the last of prizes, pensions, husbands, wives, babies, millions, appended paragraphs, and cheerful remarks. Another still would say that it means being full of incident and movement, so that we shall wish to jump ahead, to see who was the mysterious stranger, and if the stolen will was ever found, and shall not be distracted from this pleasure by any tiresome analysis or 'description.' But they would all agree that the 'artistic' idea would spoil some of their fun. One would hold it accountable for all the description, another would see it revealed in the absence of sympathy. Its hostility to a happy ending would be evident, and it might even in some cases render any ending at all impossible. The 'ending' of a novel is, for many persons, like that of a good dinner, a course of dessert and ices, and the artist in fiction is regarded as a sort of meddlesome doctor who forbids agreeable aftertastes. It is therefore true that this conception of Mr. Besant's of the novel as a superior form encounters not only a negative but a positive indifference. It matters little that as a work of art it should really be as little or as much of its essence to supply happy endings, sympathetic characters, and an objective tone, as if it were a work of mechanics: the association of ideas, however incongruous, might easily be too much for it if an eloquent voice were not sometimes raised to call attention to the fact that it is at once as free and as serious a branch of literature as any other.

Certainly this might sometimes be doubted in presence of the enormous number of works of fiction that appeal to the credulity of our generation, for it might easily seem that there could be no great character in a commodity so quickly and easily produced. It must be admitted that good novels are much compromised by bad ones, and that the field at large suffers discredit from over-crowding. I think, however, that this injury is only superficial, and that the superabundance of written fiction proves nothing against the principle itself. It has been vulgarized, like all other kinds of literature, like everything else to-day, and it has proved more than some kinds accessible to vulgarization. But there is as much difference as there ever was between a good novel and a bad one: the bad is swept with all the daubed canvases and spoiled marble into some unvisited limbo, or infinite rubbish-yard beneath the back-windows of the world, and the good subsists and emits its light and stimulates our desire for perfection. As I shall take the liberty of making but a single criticism of Mr. Besant, whose tone is so full of the love of his art, I may as well have done with it at once. He seems to me to mistake in attempting to say so definitely beforehand what sort of an affair the good novel will be. To indicate the danger of such an error as that has been the purpose of these few pages; to suggest that certain traditions on the subject, applied *a priori,* have already had much to answer for, and that the good health of an art which undertakes so immediately to reproduce life must demand that it be perfectly free. It lives upon exercise, and the very meaning of exercise is freedom. The only obligation to which in advance we may hold a novel, without incurring the accusation of being arbitrary, is that it be interesting. That general responsibility rests upon it, but it is the only one I can think of. The ways in which it is at liberty to accomplish this result (of interesting us) strike me as innumerable, and such as can only suffer from being marked out or fenced in by prescription. They are as various as the temperament of man, and they are successful in proportion as they reveal a particular mind, different from others. A novel is in its broadest definition a personal, a direct impression of life: that, to begin with, constitutes its value, which is greater or less according to the intensity of the impression. But there will be no intensity at all, and therefore no value, unless there is freedom to feel and say. The tracing of a line to be followed, of a tone to be taken, of a form to be filled out, is a limitation of that freedom and a suppression of the very thing that we are most curious about. The form, it seems to me, is to be appreciated after the fact: then the author's choice has been made, his standard has been indicated; then we can follow lines and directions and compare tones and resemblances. Then in a word we can enjoy one of the most charming of pleasures, we can estimate quality, we can apply the test of execution. The execution belongs to the author alone; it is what is most personal to him, and we measure him by that. The advantage, the luxury, as well as the torment and responsibility of the novelist, is that there is no limit to what he may attempt as an executant—no limit to his possible experiments, efforts, discoveries, successes. Here it is especially that he works, step by step, like his brother of the brush, of whom we may always say that he has painted his picture in a manner best known to himself. His manner is his secret, not necessarily a jealous one. He cannot disclose it as a general thing if he would; he would be at a loss to teach it to others. I say this with a due recollection of having insisted on the community of method of the artist who paints a picture and the artist who writes a novel. The painter *is* able to teach the rudiments of his practice, and it is possible, from the study of good work (granted the aptitude), both to learn how to paint and to learn how to write. Yet it remains true, without injury to the *rapprochement*, that the literary artist would be obliged to say to his pupil much more than the other, 'Ah, well, you must do it as you can!' It is a question of degree, a matter of delicacy. If there are exact sciences, there are also exact arts, and the grammar of painting is so much more definite that it makes the difference.

I ought to add, however, that if Mr. Besant says at the beginning of his essay that the 'laws of fiction may be laid down and taught with as much precision and exactness as the laws of harmony, perspective, and proportion,' he mitigates what might appear to be an extravagance by applying his remark to 'general' laws, and by expressing most of these rules in a manner with which it would certainly be unaccommodating to disagree. That the novelist must write from his experience, that his 'characters must be real and such as might be met with in actual life'; that 'a young lady brought up in a quiet country village should avoid descriptions of garrison life,' and 'a writer whose friends and personal experiences belong to the lower middle-class should carefully avoid introducing his characters into society'; that one should enter one's notes in a common-place book; that one's figures should be clear in outline; that making them clear by some trick of speech or of carriage is a bad method, and 'describing them at length' is a worse one; that English Fiction should have a 'conscious moral purpose'; that 'it is almost impossible to estimate too highly the value of careful workmanship—that is, of style'; that 'the most important point of all is the story,' that 'the story is everything': these are principles with most of which it is surely impossible not to sympathize. That remark about the lower middle-class writer and his knowing his place is perhaps rather chilling; but for the rest I should find it difficult to dissent from any one of these recommendations. At the same time, I should find it difficult positively to assent to them, with the exception, perhaps, of the injunction as to entering one's notes in a common-place book. They scarcely seem to me to have the quality that Mr. Besant attributes to the rules of the novelist— the 'precision and exactness' of 'the laws of harmony, perspective, and proportion.' They are suggestive, they are even inspiring, but they are not exact, though they are doubtless as much so as the case admits of: which is a proof of that liberty of interpretation for which I just contended. For the value of these different injunctions—so beautiful and so vague—is wholly in the meaning one attaches to them. The characters, the situation, which strike one as real will be those that touch and interest one most, but the measure of reality is very difficult to fix. The reality of Don Quixote or of Mr. Micawber is a very delicate shade; it is a reality so coloured by the author's vision that, vivid as it may be, one would hesitate to propose it as a model: one would expose one's self to some very embarrassing questions on the part of a pupil. It goes without saying that you will not write a good novel unless you possess the sense of reality; but it will be difficult to give you a recipe for calling that sense into being. Humanity is immense, and reality has a myriad forms; the most one can affirm is that some of the flowers of fiction have the odour of it, and others have not; as for telling you in advance how your nose-gay should be composed, that is another affair. It is equally excellent and inconclusive to say that one must write from experience; to our supposititious aspirant such a declaration might savour of mockery. What kind of experience is intended, and where does it begin and end? Experience is never limited, and it is never complete; it is an immense sensibility, a kind of huge spider-web of the finest silken threads suspended in the chamber of consciousness, and catching every air-borne particle in its tissue. It is the very atmosphere of the mind; and when the mind is imaginative—much more when it happens to be that of a man of genius—it takes to itself the faintest hints of life, it converts the very pulses of the air into revelations. The young lady living in a village has only to be a damsel upon whom nothing is lost to make it quite unfair (as it seems to me) to declare to her that she shall have nothing to say about the military. Greater miracles have been seen than that, imagination assisting, she should speak the truth about some of these gentlemen. I remember an English novelist, a woman of genius, telling me that she was much commended for the impression she had managed to give in one of her tales of the nature and way of life of the French Protestant youth. She had been asked where she learned so much about this recondite being, she had been congratulated on her peculiar opportunities. These opportunities consisted in her having once, in Paris, as she ascended a staircase, passed an open door where, in the household of a *pasteur,* some of the young Protestants were seated at table round a finished meal. The glimpse made a picture; it lasted only a moment, but that moment was experience. She had got her direct personal impression, and she turned out her type. She knew what youth was, and what Protestantism; she also had the advantage of having seen what it was to be French, so that she converted these ideas into a concrete image and produced a reality. Above all, however, she was blessed with the faculty which when you give it an inch takes an ell, and which for the artist is a much greater source of strength than any accident of residence or of place in the social scale. The power to guess the unseen from the seen, to trace the implication of things, to judge the whole piece by the pattern, the condition of feeling life in general so completely that you are well on your way to knowing any particular corner of it—this cluster of gifts may almost be said to constitute experience, and they occur in country and in town, and in the most differing stages of education. If experience consists of impressions, it may be said that impressions *are* experience, just as (have we not seen it?) they are the very air we breathe. Therefore, if I should certainly say to a novice, 'Write from experience and experience only,' I should feel that this was rather a tantalizing monition if I were not careful immediately to add, 'Try to be one of the people on whom nothing is lost!'

I am far from intending by this to minimize the importance of exactness—of truth of detail. One can speak best from one's own taste, and I may therefore venture to say that the air of reality (solidity of specification) seems to me to be the supreme virtue of a novel—the merit on which all its other merits (including that conscious moral purpose of which Mr. Besant speaks) helplessly and submissively depend. If it be not there they are all as nothing, and if these be there, they owe their effect to the success with which the author has produced the illusion of life. The cultivation of this success, the study of this exquisite process, form, to my taste, the beginning and the end of the art of the novelist. They are his inspiration, his despair, his reward, his torment, his delight. It is here in very truth that he competes with life; it is here that he competes with his brother the painter in *his* attempt to render the look of things, the look that conveys their meaning, to catch the colour, the relief, the expression, the surface, the substance of the human spectacle. It is in regard to this that Mr. Besant is well inspired when he bids him take notes. He cannot possibly take too many, he cannot possibly take enough. All life solicits him, and to 'render' the simplest surface, to produce the most momentary illusion, is a very complicated business. His case would be easier, and the rule would be more exact, if Mr. Besant had been able to tell him what notes to take. But this, I fear, he can never learn in any manual; it is the business of his life. He has to take a great many in order to select a few, he has to work them up as he can, and even the guides and philosophers who might have most to say to him must leave him alone when it comes to the application of precepts, as we leave the painter in communion with his palette. That his characters 'must be clear in outline,' as Mr. Besant says—he feels that down to his boots; but how he shall make them so is a secret between his good angel and himself. It would be absurdly simple if he could be taught that a great deal of 'description' would make them so, or that on the contrary the absence of description and the cultivation of dialogue, or the absence of dialogue and the multiplication of 'incident,' would rescue him from his difficulties. Nothing, for instance, is more possible than that he be of a turn of mind for which this odd, literal opposition of description and dialogue, incident and description, has little meaning and light. People often talk of these things as if they had a kind of internecine distinctness, instead of melting into each other at every breath, and being intimately associated parts of one general effort of expression. I cannot imagine composition existing in a series of blocks, nor conceive, in any novel worth discussing at all, of a passage of description that is not in its intention narrative, a passage of dialogue that is not in its intention descriptive, a touch of truth of any sort that does not partake of the nature of incident, or an incident that derives its interest from any other source than the general and only source of the success of a work of art—that of being illustrative. A novel is a living thing, all one and continuous, like any other organism, and in proportion as it lives will it be found, I think, that in each of the parts there is something of each of the other parts. The critic who over the close texture of a finished work shall pretend to trace a geography of items will mark some frontiers as artificial, I fear, as any that have been known to history. There is an old-fashioned distinction between the novel of character and the novel of incident which must have cost many a smile to the intending fabulist who was keen about his work. It appears to me as little to the point as the equally celebrated distinction between the novel and the romance—to answer as little to any reality. There are bad novels and good novels, as there are bad pictures and good pictures; but that is the only distinction in which I see any meaning, and I can as little imagine speaking of a novel of character as I can imagine speaking of a picture of character. When one says picture one says of character, when one says novel one says of incident, and the terms may be transposed at will. What is character but the determination of incident? What is incident but the illustration of character? What is either a picture or a novel that is *not* of character? What else do we seek in it and find in it? It is an incident for a woman to stand up with her hand resting on a table and look out at you in a certain way; or if it be not an incident I think it will be hard to say what it is. At the same time it is an expression of character. If you say you don't see it (character in *that—allons donc!*), this is exactly what the artist who has reasons of his own for thinking he *does* see it undertakes to show you. When a young man makes up his mind that he has not faith enough after all to enter the church as he intended, that is an incident, though you may not hurry to the end of the chapter to see whether perhaps he doesn't change once more. I do not say that these are extraordinary or startling incidents. I do not pretend to estimate the degree of interest proceeding from them, for this will depend upon the skill of the painter. It sounds almost puerile to say that some incidents are intrinsically much more important than others, and I need not take this precaution after having professed my sympathy for the major ones in remarking that the only classification of the novel that I can understand is into that which has life and that which has it not.

The novel and the romance, the novel of incident and that of character—these clumsy separations appear to me to have been made by critics and readers for their own convenience, and to help them out of some of their occasional queer predicaments, but to have little reality or interest for the producer, from whose point of view it is of course that we are attempting to consider the art of fiction. The case is the same with another shadowy category which Mr. Besant apparently is disposed to set up—that of the 'modern English novel'; unless indeed it be that in this matter he has fallen into an accidental confusion of standpoints.

It is not quite clear whether he intends the remarks in which he alludes to it to be didactic or historical. It is as difficult to suppose a person intending to write a modern English as to suppose him writing an ancient English novel: that is a label which begs the question. One writes the novel, one paints the picture, of one's language and of one's time, and calling it modern English will not, alas! make the difficult task any easier. No more, unfortunately, will calling this or that work of one's fellow-artist a romance—unless it be, of course, simply for the pleasantness of the thing, as for instance when Hawthorne gave this heading to his story of *Blithedale*. The French, who have brought the theory of fiction to remarkable completeness, have but one name for the novel, and have not attempted smaller things in it, that I can see, for that. I can think of no obligation to which the 'romancer' would not be held equally with the novelist; the standard of execution is equally high for each. Of course it is of execution that we are talking—that being the only point of a novel that is open to contention. This is perhaps too often lost sight of, only to produce interminable confusions and cross-purposes. We must grant the artist his subject, his idea, his *donnée*: our criticism is applied only to what he makes of it. Naturally I do not mean that we are bound to like it or find it interesting: in case we do not our course is perfectly simple—to let it alone. We may believe that of a certain idea even the most sincere novelist can make nothing at all, and the event may perfectly justify our belief; but the failure will have been a failure to execute, and it is in the execution that the fatal weakness is recorded. If we pretend to respect the artist at all, we must allow him his freedom of choice, in the face, in particular cases, of innumerable presumptions that the choice will not fructify. Art derives a considerable part of its beneficial exercise from flying in the face of presumptions, and some of the most interesting experiments of which it is capable are hidden in the bosom of common things. Gustave Flaubert has written a story about the devotion of a servant-girl to a parrot, and the production, highly finished as it is, cannot on the whole be called a success. We are perfectly free to find it flat, but I think it might have been interesting; and I, for my part, am extremely glad he should have written it; it is a contribution to our knowledge of what can be done—or what cannot. Ivan Turgénieff has written a tale about a deaf and dumb serf and a lap-dog, and the thing is touching, loving, a little masterpiece. He struck the note of life where Gustave Flaubert missed it—he flew in the face of a presumption and achieved a victory.

Nothing, of course, will ever take the place of the good old fashion of 'liking' a work of art or not liking it: the most improved criticism will not abolish that primitive, that ultimate test. I mention this to guard myself from the accusation of intimating that the idea, the subject, of a novel or a picture, does not matter. It matters, to my sense, in the highest degree, and if I might put up a prayer it would be that artists should select none but the richest. Some, as I have already hastened to admit, are much more remunerative than others, and it would be a world happily arranged in which persons intending to treat them should be exempt from confusions and mistakes. This fortunate condition will arrive only, I fear, on the same day that critics become purged from error. Meanwhile, I repeat, we do not judge the artist with fairness unless we say to him,

'Oh, I grant you your starting-point, because If I did not I should seem to prescribe to you, and heaven forbid I should take that responsibility. If I pretend to tell you what you must not take, you will call upon me to tell you then what you must take; in which case I shall be prettily caught. Moreover, it isn't till I have accepted your data that I can begin to measure you. I have the standard, the pitch; I have no right to tamper with your flute and then criticize your music. Of course I may not care for your idea at all; I may think it silly, or stale, or unclean; in which case I wash my hands of you altogether. I may content myself with believing that you will not have succeeded in being interesting, but I shall, of course, not attempt to demonstrate it, and you will be as indifferent to me as I am to you. I needn't remind you that there are all sorts of tastes: who can know it better? Some people, for excellent reasons, don't like to read about carpenters; others, for reasons even better, don't like to read about courtesans. Many object to Americans. Others (I believe they are mainly editors and publishers) won't look at Italians. Some readers don't like quiet subjects; others don't like bustling ones. Some enjoy a complete illusion, others the consciousness of large concessions. They choose their novels accordingly, and if they don't care about your idea they won't, *a fortiori*, care about your treatment.'

So that it comes back very quickly, as I have said, to the liking: in spite of M. Zola, who reasons less powerfully than he represents, and who will not reconcile himself to this absoluteness of taste, thinking that there are certain things that people ought to like, and that they can be made to like. I am quite at a loss to imagine anything (at any rate in this matter of fiction) that people *ought* to like or to dislike. Selection will be sure to take care of itself, for it has a constant motive behind it. That motive is simply experience. As people feel life, so they will feel the art that is most closely related to it. This closeness of relation is what we should never forget in talking of the effort of the novel. Many people speak of it as a factitious, artificial form, a product of ingenuity, the business of which is to alter and arrange the things that surround us, to translate them into conventional, traditional moulds. This, however, is a view of the matter which carries us but a very short way, condemns the art to an eternal repetition of a few familiar *clichés*, cuts short its development,

19

and leads us straight up to a dead wall. Catching the very note and trick, the strange irregular rhythm of life, that is the attempt whose strenuous force keeps Fiction upon her feet. In proportion as in what she offers us we see life *without* rearrangement do we feel that we are touching the truth; in proportion as we see it *with* rearrangement do we feel that we are being put off with a substitute, a compromise and convention. It is not uncommon to hear an extraordinary assurance of remark in regard to this matter of rearranging, which is often spoken of as if it were the last word of art. Mr. Besant seems to me in danger of falling into the great error with his rather unguarded talk about 'selection.' Art is essentially selection, but it is a selection whose main care is to be typical, to be inclusive. For many people art means rose-coloured window-panes, and selection means picking a bouquet for Mrs. Grundy. They will tell you glibly that artistic considerations have nothing to do with the disagreeable, with the ugly; they will rattle off shallow common-places about the prov- ince of art and the limits of art till you are moved to some wonder in return as to the province and the limits of ignorance. It appears to me that no one can ever have made a seriously artistic attempt without becoming conscious of an immense in- crease—a kind of revelation—of freedom. One perceives in that case—by the light of a heavenly ray—that the province of art is all life, all feeling, all observation, all vision. As Mr. Besant so justly intimates, it is all experience. That is a sufficient answer to those who maintain that it must not touch the sad things of life, who stick into its divine unconscious bosom little prohibitory inscriptions on the end of sticks, such as we see in public gardens —'It is forbidden to walk on the grass; it is forbidden to touch the flowers; it is not allowed to introduce dogs or to remain after dark; it is requested to keep to the right.' The young aspirant in the line of fiction whom we continue to imagine will do noth- ing without taste, for in that case his freedom would be of little use to him; but the first advantage of his taste will be to reveal to him the absurdity of the little sticks and tickets. If he have taste, I must add, of course he will have ingenuity, and my disrespectful reference to that quality just now was not meant to imply that it is useless in fiction. But it is only a secondary aid; the first is a capacity for receiving straight impressions.

Mr. Besant has some remarks on the question of 'the story' which I shall not attempt to criticize, though they seem to me to contain a singular ambiguity, because I do not think I understand them. I cannot see what is meant by talking as if there were a part of a novel which is the story and part of it which for mystical reasons is not—unless indeed the distinction be made in a sense in which it is difficult to suppose that any one should attempt to convey anything. 'The story,' if it represents anything, represents the subject, the idea, the *donnée* of the novel; and there is surely no 'school'—Mr. Besant speaks of a school—which urges that a novel should be all treatment and no subject. There must assuredly be something to treat; every school is intimately conscious of that. This sense of the story being the idea, the starting-point, of the novel, is the only one that I see in which it can be spoken of as something different from its organic whole; and since in proportion as the work is successful the idea permeates and penetrates it, informs and animates it, so that every word and every punctuation-point contribute directly to the expression, in that proportion do we lose our sense of the story being a blade which may be drawn more or less out of its sheath. The story and the novel, the idea and the form, are the needle and thread, and I never heard of a guild of tailors who recommended the use of the thread without the needle, or the needle without the thread. Mr. Besant is not the only critic who may be observed to have spoken as if there were certain things in life which constitute stories, and certain others which do not. I find the same odd implication in an entertaining article in the *Pall*

Mall Gazette, devoted, as it happens, to Mr. Besant's lecture. 'The story is the thing!' says this graceful writer, as if with a tone of opposition to some other idea. I should think it was, as every painter who, as the time for 'sending in' his picture looms in the distance, finds himself still in quest of a subject—as every belated artist not fixed about his theme will heartily agree. There are some subjects which speak to us and others which do not, but he would be a clever man who should undertake to give a rule— an *index expurgatorius*—by which the story and the no-story should be known apart. It is impossible (to me at least) to imagine any such rule which shall not be altogether arbitrary. The writer in the *Pall Mall* opposes the delightful (as I suppose) novel of *Margot la Balafrée* to certain tales in which 'Bostonian nymphs' appear to have 'rejected English dukes for psychological reasons.' I am not acquainted with the romance just designated, and can scarcely forgive the *Pall Mall* critic for not mentioning the name of the author, but the title appears to refer to a lady who may have received a scar in some heroic adventure. I am inconsolable at not being acquainted with this episode, but am utterly at a loss to see why it is a story when the rejection (or acceptance) of a duke is not, and why a reason, psychological or other, is not a subject when a cicatrix is. They are all particles of the multitudinous life with which the novel deals, and surely no dogma which pretends to make it lawful to touch the one and unlawful to touch the other will stand for a moment on its feet. It is the special picture that must stand or fall, according as it seem to possess truth or to lack it. Mr. Besant does not, to my sense, light up the subject by intimating that a story must, under penalty of not being a story, consist of 'adventures.' Why of adventures more than of green spectacles? He mentions a category of impossible things, and among them he places 'fiction without adventure.' Why without adventure, more than without matrimony, or celibacy, or parturition, or cholera, or hydropathy, or Jansenism? This seems to me to bring the novel back to the hapless little *rôle* of being an artificial, ingenious thing—bring it down from its large, free character of an immense and exquisite correspondence with life. And what *is* adventure, when it comes to that, and by what sign is the listening pupil to recognize it? It is an adventure—an immense one—for me to write this little article; and for a Bostonian nymph to reject an English duke is an adventure only less stirring, I should say, than for an English duke to be rejected by a Bostonian nymph. I see dramas within dramas in that, and innumerable points of view. A psychological reason is, to my imagination, an object adorably pictorial; to catch the tint of its complexion—I feel as if that idea might inspire one to Titianesque efforts. There are few things more exciting to me, in short, than a psychological reason, and yet, I protest, the novel seems to me the most magnificent form of art. I have just been reading, at the same time, the delightful story of *Treasure Island,* by Mr. Robert Louis Stevenson and, in a manner less consecutive, the last tale from M. Edmond de Goncourt, which is entitled *Chérie.* One of these works treats of murders, mysteries, islands of dreadful renown, hairbreadth escapes, miraculous coincidences and buried doubloons. The other treats of a little French girl who lived in a fine house in Paris, and died of wounded sensibility because no one would marry her. I call *Treasure Island* delightful, because it appears to me to have succeeded wonderfully in what it attempts; and I venture to bestow no epithet upon *Chérie,* which strikes me as having failed deplorably in what it attempts—that is in tracing the development of the moral consciousness of a child. But one of these productions strikes me as exactly as much of a novel as the other, and as having a 'story' quite as much. The moral consciousness of a child is as much a part of life as the islands of the Spanish Main, and the one sort of geography seems to me to have those 'surprises' of which Mr. Besant speaks quite as much as the other.

23

For myself (since it comes back in the last resort, as I say, to the preference of the individual), the picture of the child's experience has the advantage that I can at successive steps (an immense luxury, near to the 'sensual pleasure' of which Mr. Besant's critic in the *Pall Mall* speaks) say Yes or No, as it may be, to what the artist puts before me. I have been a child in fact, but I have been on a quest for a buried treasure only in supposition, and it is a simple accident that with M. de Goncourt I should have for the most part to say No. With George Eliot, when she painted that country with a far other intelligence, I always said Yes.

The most interesting part of Mr. Besant's lecture is unfortunately the briefest passage—his very cursory allusion to the 'conscious moral purpose' of the novel. Here again it is not very clear whether he be recording a fact or laying down a principle; it is a great pity that in the latter case he should not have developed his idea. This branch of the subject is of immense importance, and Mr. Besant's few words point to considerations of the widest reach, not to be lightly disposed of. He will have treated the art of fiction but superficially who is not prepared to go every inch of the way that these considerations will carry him. It is for this reason that at the beginning of these remarks I was careful to notify the reader that my reflections on so large a theme have no pretension to be exhaustive. Like Mr. Besant, I have left the question of the morality of the novel till the last, and at the last I find I have used up my space. It is a question surrounded with difficulties, as witness the very first that meets us, in the form of a definite question, on the threshold. Vagueness, in such a discussion, is fatal, and what is the meaning of your morality and your conscious moral purpose? Will you not define your terms and explain how (a novel being a picture) a picture can be either moral or immoral? You wish to paint a moral picture or carve a moral statue: will you not tell us how you would set about it? We are discussing the Art of Fiction; questions of art are questions (in the widest sense) of execution; questions of morality are quite another affair, and will you not let us see how it is that you find it so easy to mix them up? These things are so clear to Mr. Besant that he has deduced from them a law which he sees embodied in English Fiction, and which is 'a truly admirable thing and a great cause for congratulation.' It is a great cause for congratulation indeed when such thorny problems become as smooth as silk. I may add that in so far as Mr. Besant perceives that in point of fact English Fiction has addressed itself preponderantly to these delicate questions he will appear to many people to have made a vain discovery. They will have been positively struck, on the contrary, with the moral timidity of the usual English novelist; with his (or with her) aversion to face the difficulties with which on every side the treatment of reality bristles. He is apt to be extremely shy (whereas the picture that Mr. Besant draws is a picture of boldness), and the sign of his work, for the most part, is a cautious silence on certain subjects. In the English novel (by which of course I mean the American as well), more than in any other, there is a traditional difference between that which people know and that which they agree to admit that they know, that which they see and that which they speak of, that which they feel to be a part of life and that which they allow to enter into literature. There is the great difference, in short, between what they talk of in conversation and what they talk of in print. The essence of moral energy is to survey the whole field, and I should directly reverse Mr. Besant's remark and say not that the English novel has a purpose, but that it has a diffidence. To what degree a purpose in a work of art is a source of corruption I shall not attempt to inquire; the one that seems to me least dangerous is the purpose of making a perfect work. As for our novel, I may say lastly on this score that as we find it in England to-day it strikes me as addressed in a large degree to 'young people,' and that this in itself constitutes a presumption that it will be rather shy. There are certain things which it is generally agreed not to discuss, not even to mention, before young people. That is very well, but the absence of discussion is not a symptom of the moral passion. The purpose of the English novel—'a truly admirable thing, and a great cause for congratulation'—strikes me therefore as rather negative.

There is one point at which the moral sense and the artistic sense lie very near together; that is in the light of the very obvious truth that the deepest quality of a work of art will always be the quality of the mind of the producer. In proportion as that intelligence is fine will the novel, the picture, the statue partake of the substance of beauty and truth. To be constituted of such elements is, to my vision, to have purpose enough. No good novel will ever proceed from a superficial mind; that seems to me an axiom which, for the artist in fiction, will cover all needful moral ground: if the youthful aspirant take it to heart it will illuminate for him many of the mysteries of 'purpose.' There are many other useful things that might be said to him, but I have come to the end of my article, and can only touch them as I pass. The critic in the *Pall Mall Gazette*, whom I have already quoted, draws attention to the danger, in speaking of the art of fiction, of generalizing. The danger that he has in mind is rather, I imagine, that of particularizing, for there are some comprehensive remarks which, in addition to those embodied in Mr. Besant's suggestive lecture, might without fear of misleading him be addressed to the ingenuous student. I should remind him first of the magnificence of the form that is open to him, which offers to sight so few restrictions and such innumerable opportunities. The other arts, in comparison, appear confined and hampered; the various conditions under which they are exercised are so rigid and definite. But the only condition that I can think of attaching to the composition of the novel is, as I have already said, that it be sincere.

This freedom is a splendid privilege, and the first lesson of the young novelist is to learn to be worthy of it.

'Enjoy it as it deserves [I should say to him]; take possession of it, explore it to its utmost extent, publish it, rejoice in it. All life belongs to you, and do not listen either to those who would shut you up into corners of it and tell you that it is only here and there that art inhabits, or to those who would persuade you that this heavenly messenger wings her way outside of life altogether, breathing a superfine air, and turning away her head from the truth of things. There is no impression of life, no manner of seeing it and feeling it, to which the plan of the novelist may not offer a place; you have only to remember that talents so dissimilar as those of Alexandre Dumas and Jane Austen, Charles Dickens and Gustave Flaubert have worked in this field with equal glory. Do not think too much about optimism and pessimism; try and catch the colour of life itself. In France to-day we see a prodigious effort (that of Emile Zola, to whose solid and serious work no explorer of the capacity of the novel can allude without respect), we see an extraordinary effort vitiated by a spirit of pessimism on a narrow basis. M. Zola is magnificent, but he strikes an English reader as ignorant; he has an air of working in the dark; if he had as much light as energy, his results would be of the highest value. As for the aberrations of a shallow optimism, the ground (of English fiction especially) is strewn with their brittle particles as with broken glass. If you must indulge in conclusions, let them have the taste of a wide knowledge. Remember that your first duty is to be as complete as possible—to make as perfect a work. Be generous and delicate and pursue the prize.'

2

Preface to The Nigger of the 'Narcissus'

BY JOSEPH CONRAD

A work that aspires, however humbly, to the condition of art should carry its justification in every line. And art itself may be defined as a single-minded attempt to render the highest kind of justice to the visible universe, by bringing to light the truth, manifold and one, underlying its every aspect. It is an attempt to find in its forms, in its colors, in its light, in its shadows, in the aspects of matter and in the facts of life, what of each is fundamental, what is enduring and essential—their one illuminating and convincing quality—the very truth of their existence. The artist, then, like the thinker or the scientist, seeks the truth and makes his appeal. Impressed by the aspect of the world the thinker plunges into ideas, the scientist into facts—whence, presently, emerging they make their appeal to those qualities of our being that fit us best for the hazardous enterprise of living. They speak authoritatively to our common sense, to our intelligence, to our desire of peace or to our desire of unrest; not seldom to our prejudices, sometimes to our fears, often to our egoism—but always to our credulity. And their words are heard with reverence, for their concern is with weighty matters: with the cultivation of our minds and the proper care of our bodies, with the attainment of our ambitions, with the perfection of the means and the glorification of our precious aims.

It is otherwise with the artist.

Confronted by the same enigmatical spectacle the artist descends within himself, and in that lonely region of stress and strife, if he be deserving and fortunate, he finds the terms of his appeal. His appeal is made to our less obvious capacities: to that part of our nature which, because of the warlike conditions of existence, is necessarily kept out of sight within the more resisting and hard qualities—like the vulnerable body within a steel armor. His appeal is less loud, more profound, less distinct, more stirring—and sooner forgotten. Yet its effect endures forever. The changing wisdom of successive generations discards ideas, questions facts, demolishes theories. But the artist appeals to that part of our being which is not dependent on wisdom: to that in us which is a gift and not an acquisition—and, therefore, more permanently enduring. He speaks to our capacity for delight and wonder, to the sense of mystery surrounding our lives; to our sense of pity, and beauty, and pain; to the latent feeling of fellowship with all creation—and to the subtle but invincible conviction of solidarity that knits together the loneliness of innumerable hearts, to the solidarity in dreams, in joy, in sorrow, in aspirations, in illusions, in hope, in fear, which binds men to each other, which binds together all humanity—the dead to the living and the living to the unborn.

It is only some such train of thought, or rather of feeling, that can in a measure explain the aim of the attempt, made in the tale which follows, to present an unrestful episode in the obscure lives of a few individuals out of all the disregarded multitude of the bewildered, the simple and the voiceless. For, if any part of truth dwells in the belief confessed above, it becomes evident that there is not a place of splendor or a dark corner of the earth that does not deserve if only a passing glance of wonder and pity. The motive then, may be held to justify the matter of the work; but this preface, which is simply an avowal of endeavor, cannot end here—for the avowal is not yet complete.

Fiction—if it at all aspires to be art—appeals to temperament. And in truth it must be, like painting, like music, like all art, the appeal of one temperament to all the other innumerable temperaments whose subtle and resistless power endows passing events with their true meaning, and creates the moral, the emotional, atmosphere of the place and time. Such an appeal to be effective must be an impression conveyed through the senses; and, in fact, it cannot be made in any other way, because temperament, whether individual or collective, is not amenable to persuasion. All art, therefore, appeals primarily to the senses, and the artistic aim when expressing itself in written words must also make its appeal through the senses, if its high desire is to reach the secret spring of responsive emotions. It must strenuously aspire to the plasticity of sculpture, to the color of painting, and to the magic suggestiveness of music—which is the art of arts. And it is only through complete, unswerving devotion to the perfect blending of form and substance; it is only through an unremitting never-discouraged care for the shape and ring of sentences that an approach can be made to plasticity, to color, and that the light of magic suggestiveness may be brought to play for an evanescent instant over the commonplace surface of words: of the old, old words, worn thin, defaced by ages of careless usage.

The sincere endeavor to accomplish that creative task, to go as far on that road as his strength will carry him, to go undeterred by faltering, weariness or reproach, is the only valid justification for the worker in prose. And if his conscience is clear, his answer to those who in the fullness of a wisdom which looks for immediate profit, demand specifically to be edified, consoled, amused; who demand to be promply improved, or encouraged, or frightened, or shocked, or charmed, must run thus: My task which I am trying to achieve is, by the power of the written word to make you hear, to make you feel—it is, before all, to make you see. That—and no more, and it is everything. If I succeed, you shall find there according to your deserts: encouragement, consolation, fear, charm—all you demand—and, perhaps, also that glimpse of truth for which you have forgotten to ask.

To snatch in a moment of courage, from the remorseless rush of time, a passing phase of life, is only the beginning of the task. The task approached in tenderness and faith is to hold up unquestioningly, without choice and without fear, the rescued fragment before all eyes in the light of a sincere mood. It is to show its vibration, its color, its form; and through its movement, its form, and its color, reveal the substance of its truth—disclose its inspiring secret: the stress and passion within the core of each convincing moment. In a singleminded attempt of that kind, if one be deserving and fortunate, one may perchance attain to such clearness of sincerity that at last the presented vision of regret or pity, of terror or mirth, shall awaken in the hearts of the beholders that feeling of unavoidable solidarity; of the solidarity in mysterious origin, in toil, in joy, in hope, in uncertain fate, which binds men to each other and all mankind to the visible world.

It is evident that he who, rightly or wrongly, holds by the convictions expressed above cannot be faithful to any one of the temporary formulas of his craft The enduring part of them— the truth which each only imperfectly veils—should abide with him as the most precious of his possessions, but they all: Realism, Romanticism, Naturalism, even the unofficial sentimentalism (which like the poor, is exceedingly difficult to get rid of), all these gods must, after a short period of fellowship, abandon him —even on the very threshold of the temple—to the stammerings of his conscience and to the outspoken consciousness of the difficulties of his work. In that uneasy solitude the supreme cry of Art for Art itself loses the exciting ring of its apparent immorality. It sounds far off. It has ceased to be a cry, and is heard only as a whisper, often incomprehensible, but at times and faintly encouraging.

Sometimes, stretched at ease in the shade of a roadside tree, we watch the motions of a laborer in a distant field, and, after a time, begin to wonder languidly as to what the fellow may be at. We watch the movements of his body, the waving of his arms, we see him bend down, stand up, hesitate, begin again. It may add to the charm of an idle hour to be told the purpose of his exertions. If we know he is trying to lift a stone, to dig a ditch, to uproot a stump, we look with a more real interest at his efforts; we are disposed to condone the jar of his agitation upon the restfulness of the landscape; and even, if in a brotherly frame of mind, we may bring ourselves to forgive his failure. We understood his object, and, after all, the fellow has tried, and perhaps he had not the strength—and perhaps he had not the knowledge. We forgive, go on our way—and forget.

And so it is with the workman of art. Art is long and life is short, and success is very far off. And thus, doubtful of strength to travel so far, we talk a little about the aim—the aim of art, which, like life itself, is inspiring, difficult—obscured by mists. It is not in the clear logic of a triumphant conclusion; it is not in the unveiling of one of those heartless secrets which are called the Laws of Nature. It is not less great, but only more difficult.

To arrest, for the space of a breath, the hands busy about the work of the earth, and compel men entranced by the sight of distant goals to glance for a moment at the surrounding vision of form and color, of sunshine and shadows; to make them pause for a look, for a sigh, for a smile—such is the aim, difficult and evanescent, and reserved only for a very few to achieve. But sometimes, by the deserving and the fortunate, even that task is accomplished. And when it is accomplished—behold!—all the truth of life is there: a moment of vision, a sigh, a smile—and the return to an eternal rest.

3

Notes on Writing a Novel

BY ELIZABETH BOWEN

PLOT—*Essential. The Pre-Essential.*

Plot might seem to be a matter of choice. It is not. The particular plot is something the novelist is driven to. It is what is left after the whittling-away of alternatives. The novelist is confronted, at a moment (or at what appears to be the moment: actually its extension may be indefinite) by the impossibility of saying what is to be said in any other way.

He is forced towards his plot. By what? By the 'what is to be said.' What is 'what is to be said?' A mass of subjective matter that has accumulated—impressions received, feelings about experience, distorted results of ordinary observation, and something else—*x*. This matter is *extra* matter. It is superfluous to the non-writing life of the writer. It is luggage left in the hall between two journeys, as opposed to the perpetual furniture of rooms. It is destined to be elsewhere. It cannot move till its destination is known. Plot is the knowing of destination.

Plot is diction. Action of language, language of action.

Plot is story. It is also 'a story' in the nursery sense = lie. The novel lies, in saying that something happened that did not. It must, therefore, contain uncontradictable truth, to warrant the original lie.

Story involves action. Action towards an end not to be foreseen (by the reader) but also towards an end which, having *been* reached, must be seen to have been from the start inevitable.

Action by whom? The Characters (see CHARACTERS). Action in view of what, and because of what? The 'what is to be said.'

What about the idea that the function of action is to *express* the characters? This is wrong. The characters are there to provide the action. Each character is created, and must only be so created, as to give his or her action (or rather, contributory part in the novel's action) verisimilitude.

What about the idea that plot should be ingenious, complicated—a display of ingenuity remarkable enough to command attention? If more than such a display, what? Tension, or mystification towards tension, are good for emphasis. For their own sakes, bad.

Plot must further the novel towards its object. What object? The non-poetic statement of a poetic truth.

Have not all poetic truths been already stated? The essence of a poetic truth is that no statement of it can be final.

Plot, story, is in itself un-poetic. At best it can only be not anti-poetic. It cannot claim a single poetic licence. It must be reasoned—onward from the moment when its non-otherness, its only-possibileness has become apparent. Novelist must always have one foot, sheer circumstantiality, to stand on, whatever the other foot may be doing. (*N.B.*—Much to be learnt from story-telling to children. Much to be learnt from the detective story—especially non-irrelevance. (See RELEVANCE))

Flaubert's '*Il faut intéresser.*' Stress on manner of telling: keep in mind, 'I will a tale *unfold.*' Interest of watching silk handkerchief drawn from a conjuror's watch.

Plot must not cease to move forward. (See ADVANCE.) The *actual* speed of the movement must be even. *Apparent* variations in speed are good, necessary, but there must be no actual variations in speed. To obtain those apparent variations is part of the illusion-task of the novel. Variations in texture can be made to give the effect of variations in speed. Why are *apparent* variations in speed necessary? (a) For emphasis. (b) For non-resistance, or 'give,' to the nervous time-variations of the reader. Why is *actual* evenness, non-variation, of speed necessary? For the

sake of internal evenness for its own sake. Perfection of evenness
=perfection of control. The evenness of the speed should be the
evenness inseparable from tautness. The tautness of the taut
string is equal (or even) all along and at any part of the string's
length.

CHARACTERS

Are the characters, then, to be constructed to formula—the
formula pre-decided by the plot? Are they to be drawn, cut out,
jointed, wired, in order to be manipulated for the plot?

No. There is no question as to whether this would be right
or wrong. It would be impossible. One cannot 'make' characters, only marionettes. The manipulated movement of the
marionette is not the 'action' necessary for plot. Characterless
action is not action at all, in the plot sense. It is the indivisibility of the act from the actor, and the inevitability of *that*
act on the part of *that* actor, that gives action verisimilitude.
Without that, action is without force or reason. Forceless, rea-
sonless action disrupts plot. The term 'creation of character'
(or characters) is misleading. Characters pre-exist. They are
found. They reveal themselves slowly to the novelist's perception—as might fellow-travellers seated opposite one in a very
dimly-lit railway carriage.

The novelist's perceptions of his characters take place *in the
course of the actual writing of the novel.* To an extent, the
novelist is in the same position as his reader. But his perceptions
should be always just in advance.

The ideal way of presenting character is to invite perception.

In what do the characters pre-exist? I should say, in the mass
of matter (see PLOT) that had accumulated before the inception
of the novel.

(*N.B.*—The unanswerability of the question, from an outsider: 'Are the characters in your novel invented, or are they from

35

real life?' Obviously, neither is true. The outsider's notion of 'real life' and the novelist's are hopelessly apart.)

How, then, is the pre-existing character—with its own inner spring of action, its contrarieties—to be made to play a preassigned rôle? In relation to character, or characters, once these have been contemplated, *plot* must at once seem over-rigid, arbitrary.

What about the statement (in relation to PLOT) that 'each character is created in order, and only in order, that he or she may supply the required action?' To begin with, strike out 'created.' Better, the character is *recognized* (by the novelist) by the signs he or she gives of unique capacity to act in a certain way, which 'certain way' fulfils a need of the plot.

The character is there (in the novel) for the sake of the action he or she is to contribute to the plot. Yes. But also, he or she exists *outside* the action being contributed to the plot.

Without that existence of the character outside the (necessarily limited) action, the action itself would be invalid.

Action is the simplification (for story purposes) of complexity. For each one act, there are an x number of rejected alternatives. It is the palpable presence of the alternatives that gives action interest. Therefore, in each of the characters, while he or she is acting, the play and pull of alternatives must be felt. It is in being seen to be capable of alternatives that the character becomes, for the reader, valid.

Roughly, the action of a character should be unpredictable before it has been shown, inevitable when it has been shown. In the first half of a novel, the unpredictability should be the more striking. In the second half, the inevitability should be the more striking.

(Most exceptions to this are, however, masterpiece-novels. In *War and Peace, L'Education Sentimentale* and *La Recherche du Temps Perdu,* unpredictability dominates up to the end.)

The character's prominence in the novel (pre-decided by the plot) decides the character's range—of alternatives. The novelist must allot (to the point of rationing) psychological space. The 'hero,' 'heroine' and 'villain' (if any) are, by agreement, allowed most range. They are entitled, for the portrayal of their alternatives, to time and space. Placing the characters in receding order to their importance to the plot, the number of their alternatives may be seen to diminish. What E. M. Forster has called the 'flat' character has no alternatives at all.

The ideal novel is without 'flat' characters.

Characters must *materialize—i.e.,* must have a palpable physical reality. They must be not only see-able (visualizable); they must be to be felt. Power to give physical reality is probably a matter of the extent and nature of the novelist's physical sensibility, or susceptibility. In the main, English novelists are weak in this, as compared to French and Russians. Why?

Hopelessness of categoric 'description.' Why? Because this is static. Physical personality belongs to action: cannot be separated from it. Pictures must be in movement. Eyes, hands, stature, etc., must appear, and only appear, *in play*. Reaction to physical personality is part of action—love, or sexual passages, only more marked application of this general rule.

(Conrad an example of strong, non-sexual use of physical personality.)

The materialization (in the above sense) of the character for the novelist must be instantaneous. It happens. No effort of will —and obviously no effort of intellect—can induce it. The novelist can *use* a character that has not yet materialized. But the unmaterialized character represents an enemy pocket in an area that has been otherwise cleared. This cannot go on for long. It produces a halt in plot.

When the materialization *has* happened, the chapters written before it happened will almost certainly have to be recast. From the plot point of view, they will be found invalid.

Also, it is essential that for the reader the materialization of the character should begin early. I say begin, because for the *reader* it may, without harm, be gradual.

Is it from this failure, or tendency to fail, in materialization that the English novelist depends so much on engaging emotional sympathy for his characters?

Ruling sympathy out, a novel must contain at least one *magnetic* character. At least one character capable of keying the reader up, as though he (the reader) were in the presence of someone he is in love with. This is not a rule of salesmanship but a pre-essential of *interest*. The character must do to the reader what he has done to the novelist—magnetize towards himself perceptions, sense-impressions, desires.

The unfortunate case is, where the character has, obviously, acted magnetically upon the author, but fails to do so upon the reader.

There must be combustion. Plot depends for its movement on internal combustion.

Physically, characters are almost always copies, or composite copies. Traits, gestures, etc., are searched for in, and assembled from, the novelist's memory. Or, a picture, a photograph or the cinema screen may be drawn on. Nothing physical can be *invented*. (Invented physique stigmatizes the inferior novel.) Proust (in last volume) speaks of this assemblage of traits. Though much may be lifted from a specific person in 'real life,' no person in 'real life' could supply everything (physical) necessary for the character in the novel. No such person could have just that exact degree of physical intensity required for the character.

Greatness of characters is the measure of the unconscious greatness of the novelist's vision. They are 'true' in so far as he is occupied with poetic truth. Their degrees in realness show the degrees of his concentration.

SCENE—*Is a derivative of Plot. Gives actuality to Plot.*

Nothing can happen nowhere. The locale of the happening always colours the happening, and often, to a degree, shapes it.

Plot having pre-decided what is to happen, scene, scenes, must be so found, so chosen, as to give the happening the desired force.

Scene, being physical, is, like the physical traits of the characters, generally a copy, or a composite copy. It, too, is assembled —out of memories which, in the first place, may have had no rational connection with one another. Again, pictures, photographs, the screen are sources of supply. Also dreams.

Almost anything drawn from 'real life'—house, town, room, park, landscape—will almost certainly be found to require *some* distortion for the purposes of the plot. Remote memories, already distorted by the imagination, are most useful for the purposes of scene. Unfamiliar or once-seen places yield more than do familiar, often-seen places.

Wholly invented scene is as unsatisfactory (thin) as wholly invented physique for a character.

Scene, much more than character, is inside the novelist's conscious power. More than any other constituent of the novel, it makes him conscious *of* his power.

This can be dangerous. The weak novelist is always, compensatorily, scene-minded. (Jane Austen's economy of scene-painting, and her abstentions from it in what might be expected contexts, could in itself be proof of her mastery of the novel.)

Scene is only justified in the novel where it can be shown, or at least felt, to act upon action or character. In fact, where it has dramatic use.

Where not intended for dramatic use, scene is a sheer slower-down. Its staticness is a dead weight. It cannot make part of the plot's movement by being shown *in play*. (Thunderstorms, the sea, landscape flying past car or railway-carriage windows are not scene but happenings.)

The deadeningness of straight and prolonged 'description' is as apparent with regard to scene as it is with regard to character. Scene must be evoked. For its details relevance (see RELEVANCE) is essential. Scene must, like the characters, not fail to materialize. In this it follows the same law—instantaneous for the novelist, gradual for the reader.

In 'setting a scene' the novelist directs, or attempts to direct, the reader's visual imagination. He must allow for the fact that the reader's memories will not correspond with his own. Or, at least, not at all far along the way.

DIALOGUE—*Must* (1) Further Plot. (2) Express Character.

Should not on any account be a vehicle for ideas for their own sake. Ideas only permissible where they provide a key to the character who expresses them.

Dialogue requires more art than does any other constituent of the novel. Art in the *celare artem* sense. Art in the trickery, self-justifying distortion sense. Why? Because dialogue must appear realistic without being so. Actual realism—the lifting, as it were, of passages from a stenographer's take-town of a 'real life' conversation—would be disruptive. Of what? Of the illusion of the novel. In 'real life' everything is diluted; in the novel everything is condensed.

What are the realistic qualities to be imitated (or faked) in novel dialogue?—Spontaneity. Artless or hit-or-miss arrival at words used. Ambiguity (speaker not sure, himself, what he means). Effect of choking (as in engine): more to be said than can come through. Irrelevance. Allusiveness. Erraticness: unpredictable course. Repercussion.

What must novel dialogue, behind mask of these faked realistic qualities, really be and do? It must be pointed, intentional, relevant. It must crystallize situation. It must express character. It must advance plot.

During dialogue, the characters confront one another. The confrontation is in itself an occasion. Each one of these occasions, throughout the novel, is unique. Since the last confrontation, something has changed, advanced. What is being said is the effect of something that has happened; at the same time, what is being said *is in itself something happening,* which will in turn, leave its effect.

Dialogue is the ideal means of showing what is between the characters. It crystallizes relationships. It *should,* ideally, so be effective as to make analysis or explanation of the relationships between the characters unnecessary.

Short of a small range of physical acts—a fight, murder, love-making—dialogue is the most vigorous and visible inter-action of which characters in a novel are capable. Speech is what the characters *do to each other.*

Dialogue provides means for the psychological materialization of the characters. It should short-circuit description of mental traits. Every sentence in dialogue should be descriptive of the character who is speaking. Idiom, tempo, and shape of each spoken sentence should be calculated by novelist, towards this descriptive end.

Dialogue is the first case of the novelist's need for notation from real life. Remarks or turns of phrase indicatory of class, age, degree of intellectual pretension, *idées reçues,* nature and strength of governing fantasy, sexual temperament, persecution-sense or acumen (fortuitous arrival at general or poetic truth) should be collected. (*N.B.*—Proust, example of this semi-conscious notation and putting to use of it.)

All the above, from *class* to *acumen,* may already have been

41

established, with regard to each character, by a direct statement by the novelist to the reader. It is still, however, the business of dialogue to show these factors, or qualities, in play.

There must be present in dialogue—*i.e.,* in each sentence spoken by each character—*either* (a) calculation, or (b) involuntary self-revelation.

Each piece of dialogue *must* be 'something happening.' Dialogue *may* justify its presence by being 'illustrative'—but this secondary use of it must be watched closely, challenged. Illustrativeness can be stretched too far. Like straight description, it then becomes static, a dead weight—halting the movement of the plot. The 'amusing' for its *own* sake, should above all be censored. So should infatuation with any idiom.

The functional use of dialogue for the plot must be the first thing in the novelist's mind. Where functional usefulness cannot be established, dialogue must be left out.

What is this functional use? That of a bridge.

Dialogue is the thin bridge which must, from time to time, carry the entire weight of the novel. Two things to be kept in mind—(a) the bridge is there to permit *advance,* (b) the bridge must be strong enough for the weight.

Failure in any one piece of dialogue is a loss, at once to the continuity and the comprehensibility of the novel.

Characters should, on the whole, be under rather than over articulate. What they *intend* to say should be more evident, more striking (because of its greater inner importance to the plot) than what they arrive at *saying*.

ANGLE

The question of *angle* comes up twice over in the novel.

Angle has two senses—(a) visual, (b) moral.

(a) *Visual Angle.*—This has been much discussed—particularly I think by Henry James. Where is the camera-eye to be located? (1) In the breast or brow of *one* of the characters? This is, of course, simplifying and integrating. But it imposes on the novel the limitations of the 'I'—whether the first person is explicitly used or not. Also, with regard to any matter that the specific character does not (cannot) know, it involves the novelist in long cumbrous passages of cogitation, speculation and guesses. *E.g.*—of any character other than the specific (or virtual) 'I' it must always be 'he appeared to feel,' 'he could be seen to see,' rather than 'he felt,' 'he saw.' (2) In the breast or brow of a succession of characters? This is better. It *must*, if used, involve very careful, considered division of the characters, by the novelist, in the *seeing* and the *seen*. Certain characters gain in importance and magnetism by being only *seen*: this makes them more romantic, fatal-seeming, sinister. In fact, no character in which these qualities are, for the plot, essential should be allowed to enter the *seeing* class. (3) In the breast or brow of omniscient storyteller (the novelist)? This, though appearing naïve, would appear best. The novelist should retain right of entry, at will, into any of the characters: their memories, sensations and thought-processes should remain his, to requisition for appropriate use. What conditions 'appropriateness'? The demands of the plot. Even so, the novelist must not lose sight of point made above—the gain in necessary effect, for some characters, of their remaining *seen*— their remaining closed, apparently, even to the omniscience of the novelist.

The cinema, with its actual camera-work, is interesting study for the novelist. In a good film, the camera's movement, angle and distance have all worked towards one thing—the fullest possible realization of the director's idea, the completest possible surrounding of the subject. Any trick is justified if it adds a statement. With both film and novel, plot is the pre-imperative. The novelist's relation to the novel is that of the director's relation to the film. The cinema, cinema-going has no doubt built up in novelists a great authoritarianism. This seems to me good.

(b) *Moral Angle.*—This too often means, pre-assumptions—social, political, sexual, national, aesthetic, and so on. These may all exist, sunk at different depths, in the same novelist. Their existence cannot fail to be palpable; and their nature determines, more than anything else, the sympatheticness or antipatheticness of a given novel to a given circle of readers.

Pre-assumptions are bad. They limit the novel to a given circle of readers. They cause the novel to act immorally *on* that given circle. (The lady asking the librarian for a 'nice' novel to take home is, virtually, asking for a novel whose pre-assumptions will be identical with her own.) Outside the given circle, a novel's pre-assumptions must invalidate it for all other readers. The increasingly bad smell of most pre-assumptions probably accounts for the growing prestige of the detective story: the detective story works on the single, and universally acceptable, pre-assumption that an act of violence is anti-social, and that the doer, in the name of injured society, must be traced.

Great novelists write without pre-assumption. They write from outside their own nationality, class or sex.

To write thus should be the ambition of any novelist who wishes to state poetic truth.

Does this mean he must have no angle, no moral view-point? No, surely. Without these, he would be (a) incapable of maintaining the *conviction* necessary for the novel; (b) incapable of *lighting* the characters, who to be seen at all must necessarily be seen in a moral light.

From what source, then, must the conviction come? and from *what* morality is to come the light to be cast on the characters?

The conviction must come from certainty of the validity of the truth the novel is to present. The 'moral light' has not, actually, a moral source; it is moral (morally powerful) according to the strength of its power of revelation. Revelation of what? The virtuousness or non-virtuousness of the action of the character. What is virtue in action? Truth in action. Truth by what ruling, in relation to what? Truth by the ruling of, and in relation to, the inherent poetic truth that the novel states.

The presence, and action, of the poetic truth is the motive (or motor) morality of the novel.

The direction of the action of the poetic truth provides—in fact, *is*—the moral angle of the novel. If he remains with that truth in view, the novelist has no option as to his angle.

The action, or continuous line of action, of a character is 'bad' in so far as it runs counter to, resists, or attempts to deny, the action of the poetic truth. It is predisposition towards such action that constitutes 'badness' in a character.

'Good' action, or 'goodness' in the character, from predisposition towards such action, is movement along with, expressive of and contributory to, the action of the poetic truth.

If the novelist's moral angle is (a) decided by recognition of the poetic truth, and (b) maintained by the necessity of stating the truth by showing the truth's action, it will be, as it should be, impersonal. It will be, and (from the 'interest' point of view) will be able to stand being, pure of pre-assumptions—national, social, sexual, etc.

(*N.B.*—'Humour' is the weak point in the front against pre-assumptions. Almost all English humour shows social (sometimes, now, backed by political) pre-assumptions. (Extreme cases —that the lower, or employed, classes are quaint or funny—that aristocrats, served by butlers, are absurd. National pre-assumptions show in treatment of foreigners.)

ADVANCE

It has been said that plot must advance; that the underlying (or inner) speed of the advance must be even. How is this arrived at?

(1) Obviously, first, by the succession, the succeedingness, of events or happenings. It is to be remembered that *everything* put on record at all—an image, a word spoken, an interior movement of thought or feeling on the part of a character—is an event or happening. These proceed out of one another, give birth to one another, in a continuity that must be (a) obvious, (b) unbroken.

(2) Every happening cannot be described, stated. The reader must be made to feel that what has not been described or stated has, none the less, happened. How? By the showing of subsequent events or happenings whose source *could* only have been in what has not actually been stated. Tuesday is Tuesday by virtue of being the day following Monday. The stated Tuesday must be shown as a derivative of the unstated Monday.

(3) For the sake of emphasis, time must be falsified. But the novelist's consciousness of the subjective, arbitrary and emotional nature of the falsification should be evident to the reader. Against this falsification—in fact, increasing the force of its effect by contrast—a clock should be heard always impassively ticking away at the same speed. The passage of time, and its demarcation, should be a factor in plot. The either concentration or even or uneven spacing-out of events along time is important.

The statement 'Ten years had passed,' or the statement 'It was now the next day'—each of these is an event.

(4) Characters most of all promote, by showing, the advance of the plot. How? By the advances, from act to act, in their action. By their showing (by emotional or physical changes) the effects both of action and of the passage of time. The diminution of the character's alternatives shows (because it is the work of) advance—by the end of a novel the character's alternatives, many

at the beginning, have been reduced to almost none. In the novel, everything that happens happens either *to* or *because* of one of the characters. By the end of the novel, the character has, like the silk worm at work on the cocoon, spun itself out. Completed action is marked by the exhaustion (from one point of view) of the character. Throughout the novel, each character is expending potentiality. This expense of potentiality must be felt.

(5) Scene promotes, or contributes to, advance by its freshness. Generically, it is fresh, striking, from being unlike the scene before. It is the new 'here and now.' Once a scene ceases to offer freshness, it is a point-blank enemy to advance. Frequent change of scene *not* being an imperative of the novel—in fact, many novels by choice, and by wise choice, limiting themselves severely in this matter—how is there to continue to be freshness? By means of ever-differing presentation. Differing because of what? Season of year, time of day, effects of a happening (*e.g.*, with house, rise or fall in family fortunes, an arrival, a departure, a death), beholding character's mood. At the first presentation, the *scene* has freshness; afterwards, the freshness must be in the *presentation*. The same scene can, by means of a series of presentations, each having freshness, be made to ripen, mature, to actually advance. The *static* properties in scene can be good for advance when so stressed as to show advance by contrast—advance on the part of the characters. Striking 'unchangingness' gives useful emphasis to change. Change should not be a factor, at once, in *both* scene and character; either unchanged character should see, or be seen against, changed scene, or changed character should see, or be seen, against unchanged scene. *Two* changes obviously cancel each other out, and would cancel each other's contribution to the advance of plot.

RELEVANCE

Relevance—the question of it—is the headache of novel-writing.

As has been said, the model for relevance is the well-constructed detective story: nothing is 'in' that does not tell. But the detective story is, or would appear to be, simplified by having *fact* as its kernel. The detective story makes towards concrete truth; the novel makes towards abstract truth.

With the detective story, the question 'relevant to *what?*' can be answered by the intelligence. With the novel, the same question must constantly, and in every context, be referred to the intuition. The intelligence, in a subsequent check over, may detect, but cannot itself put right, blunders, lapses or false starts on the part of the intuition.

In the notes on Plot, Character, Scene and Dialogue, everything has come to turn, by the end, on relevance. It is seen that all other relevances are subsidiary to the relevance of the plot— *i.e.,* the relevance to itself that the plot demands. It is as contributory, in fact relevant, to plot that characer, scene and dialogue are examined. To be perfectly contributory, these three must be perfectly relevant. If character, scene or dialogue has been weakened by anything irrelevant *to itself,* it can only be imperfectly relevant—which must mean, to a degree disruptive— to the plot.

The main hope for character (for each character) is that it should be magnetic—*i.e.,* that it should *attract* its parts. This living propensity of the character to assemble itself, to integrate itself, to make itself in order to *be* itself will not, obviously, be resisted by the novelist. The magnetic, or magnetizing, character can be trusted as to what is relevant *to itself.* The trouble comes when what is relevant to the character is found to be not relevant to the plot. At this point, the novelist must adjudicate. It is possible that the character may be right; it is possible that there may be some flaw in the novelist's sense of what is relevant to the plot.

Again, the character may, in fact must, decide one half of the question of relevance in dialogue. The character attracts to itself the right, in fact the only possible, idiom, tempo and phraseology for *that* particular character in speech. In so far as dialogue is *illustrative,* the character's, or characters', pull on it must not be resisted.

But in so far as dialogue must be 'something happening'— part of action, a means of advancing plot—the other half of the question of dialogue-relevance comes up. Here, the pull from the characters may conflict with the pull from the plot. Here again the novelist must adjudicate. The recasting and recasting of dialogue that is so often necessary is, probably, the search for ideal compromise.

Relevance in scene is more straightforward. Chiefly, the novelist must control his infatuation with his own visual power. *No* non-contributory image, must be the rule. Contributory to what? To the mood of the 'now,' the mood that either projects or reflects action. It is a good main rule that objects—chairs, trees, glasses, mountains, cushions—introduced into the novel should be stage-properties, necessary for 'business.' It will be also recalled that the well-set stage shows many objects *not* actually necessary for 'business,' but that these have a right to place by being descriptive—explanatory. In a play, the absence of the narrating voice makes it necessary to establish the class, period and general psychology of the characters by means of objects that can be seen. In the novel, such putting of objects to a descriptive (explanatory) use is excellent—alternative to the narrator's voice.

In scene then, relevance demands either usefulness for action or else explanatory power in what is shown. There is no doubt that with some writers (Balzac, sometimes Arnold Bennett) categoricalness, in the presentation of scene, is effective. The aim is, usually, to suggest, by multiplication and exactitude of detail, either a scene's material oppressiveness or its intrinsic authority. But in general, for the purposes of most novelists, the number of objects genuinely necessary for explanation will be found to be very small.

Irrelevance, in any part, is a cloud and a drag on, a weakener of, the novel. It dilutes meaning. Relevance crystallizes meaning.

The novelist's—any writer's—object is, to whittle down his meaning to the exactest and finest possible point. What, of course, is fatal is when he does not know what he does mean: he has no point to sharpen.

Much irrelevance is introduced into novels by the writer's vague hope that at least some of this *may* turn out to be relevant, after all. A good deal of what might be called provisional writing goes to the first drafts of first chapters of most novels. At a point in the novel's progress, relevance becomes clearer. The provisional chapters are then recast.

The most striking fault in work by young or beginning novelists submitted for criticism, is irrelevance—due either to infatuation or indecision. To direct such an author's attention to the imperative of relevance is certainly the most useful—and possibly the only—help that can be given.

II CRAFT AND TECHNIQUE

4

Point of View

The whole intricate question of method, in the craft of fiction,
I take to be governed by the question of the point of view—the
question of the relation in which the narrator stands to the story.
He tells it as *he* sees it, in the first place; the reader faces the story-
teller and listens, and the story may be told so vivaciously that the
presence of the minstrel is forgotten, and the scene becomes
visible, peopled with the characters of the tale. It may be so,
it very often is so for a time. But it is not so always, and the story-
teller himself grows conscious of a misgiving. If the spell is
weakened at any moment, the listener is recalled from the scene
to the mere author before him, and the story rests only upon the
author's direct assertion. Is it not possible, then, to introduce another point of view, to set up a fresh narrator to bear the brunt
of the reader's scrutiny? If the story-teller is *in* the story himself,
the author is dramatized; his assertions gain in weight, for they are
backed by the presence of the narrator in the pictured scene. It
is advantage scored; the author has shifted his responsibility, and
it now falls where the reader can see and measure it; the arbitrary quality which may at any time be detected in the author's
voice is disguised in the voice of his spokesman. Nothing is now
imported into the story from without; it is self-contained, it has
no associations with anyone beyond its circle.

Such is the first step towards dramatization, and in very many
a story it may be enough. The spokesman is there, in recognizable
relation with his matter; no question of his authority can arise.
But now a difficulty may be started by the nature of the tale that

he tells. If he has nothing to do but to relate what he has seen, what anyone might have seen in his position, his account will serve very well; there is no need for more. Let him unfold his chronicle as it appears in his memory. But if he is himself the subject of his story, if the story involves a searching exploration of his own consciousness, an account in his own words, after the fact, is not by any means the best imaginable. Far better it would be to see him while his mind is actually at work in the agitation, whatever it may be, which is to make the book. The matter would then be objective and visible to the reader, instead of reaching him in the form of a report at second hand. But how to manage this without falling back upon the author and *his* report, which has already been tried and for good reasons, as it seemed, abandoned? It is managed by a kind of repetition of the same stroke, a further shift of the point of view. The spectator, the listener, the reader, is now himself to be placed at the angle of vision; not an account or a report, more or less convincing, is to be offered him, but a direct sight of the matter itself, while it is passing. Nobody expounds or explains; the story is enacted by its look and behaviour at particular moments. By the first stroke the narrator was brought into the book and set before the reader; but the action appeared only in his narrative. Now the action is there, proceeding while the pages are turned; the narrator is forestalled, he is watched while the story is in the making. Such is the progress of the writer of fiction towards drama; such is his method of evading the drawbacks of a mere reporter and assuming the advantages, as far as possible, of a dramatist. How far he may choose to push the process in his book—that is a matter to be decided by the subject; it entirely depends upon the kind of effect that the theme demands. It may respond to all the dramatization it can get, it may give all that it has to give for less. The subject dictates the method.

And now let the process be reversed, let us start with the

purely dramatic subject, the story that will tell itself in perfect rightness, unaided, to the eye of the reader. This story never deviates from a strictly scenic form; one occasion or episode follows another, with no interruption for any reflective summary of events. Necessarily it must be so, for it is only while the episode is proceeding that no question of a narrator can arise; when the scene closes the play ceases till the opening of the next. To glance upon the story from a height and to give a general impression of its course—this is at once to remove the point of view from the reader and to set up a new one somewhere else; the method is no longer consistent, no longer purely dramatic. And the dramatic story is not only scenic, it is also limited to so much as the ear can hear and the eye see. In rigid drama of this kind there is naturally no admission of the reader into the private mind of any of the characters; their thoughts and motives are transmuted into action. A subject wrought to this pitch of objectivity is no doubt given weight and compactness and authority in the highest degree; it is like a piece of modelling, standing in clear space, casting its shadow. It is the most finished form that fiction can take.

But evidently it is not a form to which fiction can aspire in general. It implies many sacrifices, and these will easily seem to be more than the subject can usefully make. It is out of the question, of course, wherever the main burden of the story lies within some particular consciousness, in the study of a soul, the growth of a character, the changing history of a temperament; there the subject would be needlessly crossed and strangled by dramatization pushed to its limit. It is out of the question, again, wherever the story is too big, too comprehensive, too widely ranging, to be treated scenically, with no opportunity for general and panoramic survey; it has been discovered, indeed, that even a story of this kind *may* fall into a long succession of definite scenes, under some hands, but it has also appeared that in doing so it incurs unnecessary disabilities, and will likely suffer. These stories, therefore, which will not naturally accommodate themselves to the reader's point of view, and the reader's alone, we regard as rather pictorial than dramatic—meaning that they call for some narrator, somebody who *knows,* to contemplate the facts and create an impression of them. Whether it is the omniscient author or a man in the book, he must gather up his experience, compose a vision of it as it exists in his mind, and lay *that* before the reader. It is the reflection of an experience; and though there may be all imaginable diversity of treatment within the limits of the reflection, such is its essential character. In a pictorial book the principle of the structure involves a point of view which is not the reader's.

It is open to the pictorial book, however, to use a method in its picture-making that is really no other than the method of drama. It is somebody's experience, we say, that is to be reported, the general effect that many things have left upon a certain mind; it is a fusion of innumerable elements, the deposit of a lapse of time. The straightforward way to render it would be for the narrator—the author or his selected creature—to view the past retrospectively and discourse upon it, to recall and meditate and summarize. That is picture-making in its natural form, using its own method. But exactly as in drama the subject is distributed among the characters and enacted by them, so in picture the effect may be entrusted to the elements, the reactions of the moment, and *performed* by these. The mind of the narrator becomes the stage, his voice is no longer heard. His voice *is* heard so long as there is narrative of any sort, whether he is speaking in person or is reported obliquely; his voice is heard, because in either case the language and the intonation are his, the direct expression of his experience. In the drama of his mind there is no personal voice, for there is no narrator; the point of view becomes the reader's once more. The shapes of thought in the man's mind tell their own story. And that is the art of picture-making when it uses the dramatic method.

But it cannot always do so. Constantly it must be necessary to offer the reader a summary of facts, an impression of a train of events, that can only be given as somebody's narration. Suppose it were required to render the general effect of a certain year in a man's life, a year that has filled his mind with a swarm of many memories. Looking into his consciousness after the year has gone, we might find much there that would indicate the nature of the year's events without any word on his part; the flickers and flashes of thought from moment to moment might indeed tell us much. But we shall need an account from him too, no doubt; too much has happened in a year to be wholly acted, as I call it, in the movement of the man's thought. He must narrate—he must make, that is to say, a picture of the events as he sees them, glancing back. Now if he speaks in the first person there can, of course, be no uncertainty in the point of view; he has his fixed position, he cannot leave it. His description will represent the face that the facts in their sequence turned towards *him*; the field of vision is defined with perfect distinctness, and his story cannot stray outside it. The reader, then, may be said to watch a reflection of the facts in a mirror of which the edge is nowhere in doubt; it is rounded by the bounds of the narrator's own personal experience.

This limitation may have a convenience and a value in the story, it may contribute to the effect. But it need not be forfeited, it is clear, if the first person is changed to the third. The author may use the man's field of vision and keep as faithfully within it as though the man were speaking for himself. In that case he retains this advantage and adds to it another, one that is likely to be very much greater. For now, while the point of view is still fixed in space, still assigned to the man in the book, it is free in *time*; there no longer stretches, between the narrator and the events of which he speaks, a certain tract of time, across which the past must appear in a more or less distant perspective. All the variety obtainable by a shifting relation to the story in time is thus in the author's hand; the safe serenity of a far retrospect, the promising or threatening urgency of the present, every gradation between the two, can be drawn into the whole effect of the book, and all of it without any change of the seeing eye. It is a liberty that may help the story indefinitely, raising this matter into strong relief, throwing that other back into vaguer shade.

And next, still keeping mainly and ostensibly to the same point of view, the author has the chance of using a much greater latitude than he need appear to use. The seeing eye is with somebody in the book, but its vision is reinforced; the picture contains more, becomes richer and fuller, because it is the author's as well as his creature's, both at once. Nobody notices, but in fact there are now two brains behind that eye; and one of them is the author's, who adopts and shares the *position* of his creature, and at the same time supplements his wit. If you analyse the picture that is now presented, you find that it is not all the work of the personage whose vision the author has adopted. There are touches in it that go beyond any sensation of his, and indicate that some one else is looking over his shoulder—seeing things from the same angle, but seeing more, bringing another mind to bear upon the scene. It is an easy and natural extension of the personage's power of observation. The impression of the scene may be deepened as much as need be; it is not confined to the scope of one mind, and yet there is no blurring of the focus by a double point of view. And thus what I have called the sound of the narrator's voice (it is impossible to avoid this mixture of metaphors) is less insistent in oblique narration, even while it seems to be following the very same argument that it would in direct, because another voice is speedily mixed and blended with it.

So this is another resource upon which the author may draw

according to his need; sometimes it will be indispensable, and generally, I suppose, it will be useful. It means that he keeps a certain hold upon the narrator *as an object*; the sentient character in the story, round whom it is grouped, is not utterly subjective, completely given over to the business of seeing and feeling on behalf of the reader. It is a considerable point; for it helps to meet one of the great difficulties in the story which is carefully aligned towards a single consciousness and consistently so viewed. In that story the man or woman who acts as the vessel of sensation is always in danger of seeming a light, uncertain weight compared with the other people in the book—simply because the other people are objective images, plainly outlined, while the seer in the midst is precluded from that advantage, and must see without being directly seen. He, who doubtless ought to bulk in the story more massively than any one, tends to remain the least recognizable of the company, and even to dissolve in a kind of impalpable blur. By his method (which I am supposing to have been adopted in full strictness) the author is of course forbidden to look this central figure in the face, to describe and discuss him; the light cannot be turned upon him immediately. And very often we see the method becoming an embarrassment to the author in consequence, and the devices by which he tries to mitigate it, and to secure some reflected sight of the seer, may even be tiresomely obvious. But the resource of which I speak is of a finer sort.

It gives to the author the power of imperceptibly edging away from the seer, leaving his consciousness, ceasing to use his eyes—though still without substituting the eyes of another. To revert for a moment to the story told in the first person, it is plain that in that case the narrator has no such liberty; his own consciousness must always lie open; the part that he plays in the story can never appear in the same terms, on the same plane, as that of the other people. Though he is not visible in the story to the reader, as the others are, he is at every moment *nearer* than they, in his capacity of the seeing eye, the channel of vision; nor can he put off his function, he must continue steadily to see and to report. But when the author is reporting *him* there is a margin of freedom. The author has not so completely identified himself, as narrator, with his hero that he can give him no objective weight whatever. If necessary he can allow him something of the value of a detached and phenomenal personage, like the rest of the company in the story, and that without violating the principle of his method. He cannot make his hero actually visible— there the method is uncompromising; he cannot step forward, leaving the man's point of view, and picture him from without. But he can place the man at the same distance from the reader as the other people, he can almost lend him the same effect, he can make of him a dramatic actor upon the scene.

And how? Merely by closing (when it suits him) the open consciousness of the seer—which he can do without any look of awkwardness or violence, since it conflicts in no way with the rule of the method. That rule only required that the author, having decided to share the point of view of his character, should not proceed to set up another of his own; it did not debar him from allowing his hero's act of vision to lapse, his function as the sentient creature in the story to be intermitted. The hero (I call him so for convenience—he may, of course, be quite a subordinate onlooker in the story) can at any moment become impenetrable, a human being whose thought is sealed from us; and it may seem a small matter, but in fact it has the result that he drops into the plane of the people whom he has hitherto been seeing and judging. Hitherto subjective, communicative in solitude, he has been in a category apart from them; but now he may mingle with the rest, engage in talk with them, and his presence and his talk are no more to the fore than theirs. As soon as some description or discussion of them is required, then, of course, the seer must resume his part and unseal his mind; but meanwhile, though the reader gets no direct view of him, still he is there in the dialogue with the rest, his speech (like theirs) issues from a hidden mind and has the same dramatic value. It is enough, very likely, to harden our image of him, to give precision to his form, to save him from dissipation into that luminous blur of which I spoke just now. For the author it is a resource to be welcomed on that account, and not on that account alone.

For besides the greater definition that the seer acquires, thus detached from us at times and relegated to the plane of his companions, there is much benefit for the subject of the story. In the tale that is quite openly and nakedly somebody's narrative there is this inherent weakness, that a scene of true drama is impossible. In true drama nobody *reports* the scene; it *appears*, it is constituted by the aspect of the occasion and the talk and the conduct of the people. When one of the people who took part in it sets out to report the scene, there is at once a mixture and a confusion of effects; for his own contribution to the scene has a different quality from the rest, cannot have the same crispness and freshness, cannot strike in with a new or unexpected note. This weakness may be well disguised, and like everything else in the whole craft it may become a positive and right effect in a particular story, for a particular purpose; it is always there, however, and it means that the full and unmixed effect of drama is denied to the story that is rigidly told from the point of view of one of the actors. But when that point of view is held in the manner I have described, when it is open to the author to withdraw from it silently and to leave the actor to play his part, true drama—or something so like it that it passes for true drama—is always possible; all the figures of the scene are together in it, one no nearer than another. Nothing is wanting save only that direct, unequivocal sight of the hero which the method does indeed absolutely forbid.

Finally there is the old, immemorial, unguarded, unsuspicious way of telling a story, where the author entertains the reader, the minstrel draws his audience round him, the listeners rely upon his word. The voice is then confessedly and alone the author's; he imposes no limitation upon his freedom to tell what he pleases and to regard his matter from a point of view that is solely his own. And if there is anyone who can proceed in this fashion without appearing to lose the least of the advantages of a more cautious style, for him the minstrel's licence is proper and appropriate; there is no more to be said. But we have yet to discover him; and it is not very presumptuous in a critic, as things are, to declare that a story will never yield its best to a writer who takes the easiest way with it. He curtails his privileges and chooses a narrower method, and immediately the story responds; its better condition is too notable to be forgotten, when once it has caught the attention of a reader. The advantages that it gains are not nameless, indefinable graces, pleasing to a critic but impossible to fix in words; they are solid, we can describe and recount them. And I can only conclude that if the novel is still as full of energy as it seems to be, and is not a form of imaginative art that, having seen the best of its day, is preparing to give place to some other, the novelist will not be willing to miss the inexhaustible opportunity that lies in its treatment. The easy way is no way at all; the only way is that by which the most is made of the story to be told, and the most was never made of any story except by a choice and disciplined method.

5

Stream of Consciousness

BY ROBERT HUMPHREY

> *The discovery that memories, thoughts, and feelings exist outside the primary consciousness is the most important step forward that has occurred in psychology since I have been a student of that science.*

> WILLIAM JAMES

Stream of consciousness is one of the delusive terms which writers and critics use. It is delusive because it sounds concrete and yet it is used as variously—and vaguely—as "romanticism," "symbolism," and "surrealism." We never know whether it is being used to designate the bird of technique or the beast of genre—and we are startled to find the creature designated is most often a monstrous combination of the two. The purpose of this study is to examine the term and its literary implications.

Stream of Consciousness Defined

Stream of consciousness is properly a phrase for psychologists. William James coined it. The phrase is most clearly useful when it is applied to mental processes, for as a rhetorical locution it becomes doubly metaphorical; that is, the word "consciousness" as well as the word "stream" is figurative, hence, both are less precise and less stable. If, then, the term stream of consciousness (I shall use it since it is already established as a literary label) is reserved for indicating an approach to the presentation of *psy-*

chological aspects of character in fiction, it can be used with some precision. This reservation I shall make, and it is the basis from which the contradicting and often meaningless commentary on the stream-of-consciousness novel can be resolved.*

The stream-of-consciousness novel is identified most quickly by its subject matter. This, rather than its techniques, its purposes, or its themes, distinguishes it. Hence, the novels that are said to use the stream-of-consciousness *technique* to a considerable degree prove, upon analysis, to be novels which have as their essential subject matter the consciousness of one or more characters; that is, the depicted consciousness serves as a screen on which the material in these novels is presented.

"Consciousness" should not be confused with words which denote more restricted mental activities, such as "intelligence" or "memory." The justifiably irate comments of the psychology scholars deplore the layman's use of the term. One of these scholars writes: "It has been said that no philosophical term is at once so popular and so devoid of standard meaning as *consciousness*; and the layman's usage of the term has been credited with begging as many metaphysical questions as will probably be the privilege of any single word." The area which we are to examine here is an important one in which this confusion has been amassed. Since our study will concern persons who are laymen in psychology, it is necessary that we proceed with the "layman's usage." Naturally, the stream-of-consciousness writers have not defined their label. We readers who have stamped it on them must try to do it.

---

* At least two writers, Frederick Hoffman and Harry Levin, have recognized this loose use of "stream of consciousness." Levin employs in its place the French rhetorical term *monologue intérieur*. Although Levin uses even this term too loosely for any general discussion of that technique, it serves well for his special purposes. I am indebted to him for the basic distinction between the terms in question.

Consciousness indicates the entire area of mental attention, from preconsciousness on through the levels of the mind up to and including the highest one of rational, communicable awareness. This last area is the one with which almost all psychological fiction is concerned. Stream-of-consciousness fiction differs from all other psychological fiction precisely in that it is concerned with those levels that are more inchoate than rational verbalization—those levels on the margin of attention.

So far as stream-of-consciousness fiction is concerned, it is pointless to try to make definite categories of the many levels of consciousness. Such attempts demand the answers to serious metaphysical questions, and they put serious questions about the stream-of-consciousness writers' concepts of psychology and their aesthetic intentions—questions which the epistemologists, the psychologists, and the literary historians have not yet answered satisfactorily. It is desirable for an analysis of stream-of-consciousness fiction to assume that there are levels of consciousness from the lowest one just above oblivion to the highest one which is represented by verbal (or other formal) communication. "Low" and "high" simply indicate degrees of the rationally ordered. The adjectives "dim" and "bright" could be used just as well to indicate these degrees. There are, however, two levels of consciousness which can be rather simply distinguished: the "speech level" and the "prespeech level." There is a point at which they overlap, but otherwise the distinction is quite clear. The prespeech level, which is the concern of most of the literature under consideration in this study, involves no communicative basis as does the speech level (whether spoken or written). This is its salient distinguishing characteristic. In short, the prespeech levels of consciousness are not censored, rationally controlled, or logically ordered. By "consciousness," then, I shall mean the whole area of mental processes, including especially the prespeech levels. The term "psyche" I shall use as a synonym for "consciousness," and at times, even the word "mind" will serve as another synonym. These synonyms, although they are handicapped by the various evocative qualities they possess, are convenient to use because they lend themselves well to the forming of adjectives and adverbs.

Hence, "consciousness" must not be confused with "intelligence" or "memory" or any other such limiting term. Henry James has written novels which reveal psychological processes in which a single point of view is maintained so that the entire novel is presented through the intelligence of a character. But these, since they do not deal at all with prespeech levels of consciousness, are not what I have defined as stream-of-consciousness novels. Marcel Proust has written a modern classic which is often cited as an example of stream-of-consciousness fiction, but *A la recherche du temps perdu* is concerned only with the reminiscent aspect of consciousness. Proust was deliberately recapturing the past for the purposes of communication; hence he did not write a stream-of-consciousness novel. Let us think of consciousness as being in the form of an iceberg—the whole iceberg and not just the relatively small surface portion. Stream-of-consciousness fiction is, to follow this comparison, greatly concerned with what lies below the surface.

With such a concept of consciousness, we may define stream-of-consciousness fiction as a type of fiction in which the basic emphasis is placed on exploration of the prespeech levels of consciousness for the purpose, primarily, of revealing the psychic being of the characters.

When some of the novels which fall into this classification are considered, it becomes immediately apparent that the techniques by which the subjects are controlled and the characters are presented are palpably different from one novel to the next. Indeed, there is no stream-of-consciousness technique. Instead, there are several quite different techniques which are used to present stream of consciousness.

The Self-conscious Mind

It is not an uncommon misconception that many modern novels, and particularly the ones that are generally labeled stream of consciousness, rely greatly upon private symbols to represent private confusions. The misconception comes primarily from considering whatever is "internal" or "subjective" in characterization as arrant fantasy, or, at best, as psychoanalytical.* Serious misreadings and unsound evaluations result from this initial misunderstanding, particularly in discussion of major twentieth-century novels. I refer to such subjective fiction as *Ulysses, Mrs. Dalloway, To the Lighthouse,* and *The Sound and the Fury.* These novels may very well be within a category we can label stream of consciousness, so long as we know what we are talking about. The evidence reveals that we never do—or never have done so.

It is meaningless to label all of the novels stream of consciousness that are generally named as such, unless we mean by that phrase simply "inner awareness." The expression of this quality is what they have in common. It is, however, apparent that that is not what has been meant when they have been so labeled and forced to share the same categorical niche. It is not what William James meant when he coined the term. James was formulating psychological theory and he had discovered that "memories, thoughts, and feelings exist outside the primary consciousness" and, further, that they appear to one, not as a chain, but as a stream, a flow. Whoever, then, first applied the phrase to the

---

* It is, of course, true that there are several attempts to represent character in fiction in psychoanalytical terms—notably in Conrad Aiken's novels, *Blue Voyage* and *Great Circle*—but these attempts are for the most part curiosities, and they are finally insignificant.

novel did so correctly only if he was thinking of a *method* of representing inner awareness. What has actually happened is that *monologue intérieur* was clumsily translated into English. But it is palpably true that the methods of the novels in which this device is used are different, and that there are dozens of other novels which use internal monologue which no one would seriously classify as stream of consciousness. Such are, for example, *Moby Dick, Les Fauxmonnayeurs,* and *Of Time and the River.* Stream of consciousness, then, is not a synonym for *monologue intérieur.* It is not a term to name a particular method or technique; although it probably was used originally in literary criticism for that purpose. One can safely conjecture that such a loose and fanciful term was a radiant buoy to well-meaning critics who had lost their bearings. The natural, and historically accurate, association of the term with psychology, along with the overwhelming psychoanalytical trend of twentieth-century thought, has resulted in giving all novels that could be loosely associated with the loose phrase "stream of consciousness" a marked Viennese accent.

The word "stream" need not concern us immediately, for representation of the flow of consciousness is, provided one is convinced that consciousness flows, entirely a matter of technique. The approach to take is to consider the word "consciousness" and to attempt to formulate what, to the various writers, is the ultimate significance of what consciousness contains. It is, in short, a psychological and a philosophical question. Stream-of-consciousness literature is psychological literature, but it must be studied at the level on which psychology mingles with epistemology. Immediately the question confronts us: What does consciousness contain? Then, too, what does it contain so far as philosophy and psychology have investigated it *and* what does it contain so far as the novelists in question have represented it? These may be mutually exclusive questions; they are certainly different ones. But the concern here is not with psychological theory; it is with novelistic subject matter. The question for this study is a phenomenological one: What does consciousness contain in the sense of what has it contained so far as the consciousness of the novelists have experienced it? Any answer must respect the possible range of a creative writer's sensitivity and imagination. No answer needs proving beyond the gesture of saying: There it is in Virginia Woolf; there it is in James Joyce. It should be remembered that, first, we are attempting to clarify a literary term; and second, we are trying to determine how fictional art is enriched by the depiction of inner states.

The attempt to create human consciousness in fiction is a modern attempt to analyze human nature. Most of us will be convinced, now, that it can be the starting point of that most important of all intellectual functions. We have, for example, Henry James's word for it that "experience is never limited, and it is never complete." He continues in the same context to point to the "chamber of consciousness" as the chamber of experience. Consciousness, then, is *where* we are aware of human experience. And this is enough for the novelist. He, collectively, leaves nothing out: sensations and memories, feelings and conceptions, fancies and imaginations—and those very unphilosophic, but consistently unavoidable phenomena we call intuitions, visions, and insights. These last terms, which usually embarrass the epistemologist, unlike the immediately preceding series, are not always included under the label "mental life." Precisely for this reason it is important to point them up here. Human "knowledge" which comes not from "mental" activity but from "spiritual" life is a concern of novelists, if not of psychologists. Knowledge, then, as a category of consciousness must include intuition, vision, and sometimes even the occult, so far as twentieth-century writers are concerned.

Thus, we may, on inductive grounds, conclude that the realm of life with which stream-of-consciousness literature is concerned is mental and spiritual experience—both the whatness and the howness of it. The whatness includes the categories of mental experiences: sensations, memories, imaginations, conceptions, and intuitions. The howness includes the symbolizations, the feelings, and the processes of association. It is often impossible to separate the what from the how. Is, for example, memory a part of mental contènt or is it a mental process? Such fine distinctions, of course, are not the concern of novelists as novelists. Their object, if they are writing stream of consciousness, is to enlarge fictional art by depicting the inner states of their characters.

The problem of character depiction is central to stream-of-consciousness fiction. The great advantage, and consequently the best justification of this type of novel, rests on its potentialities for presenting character more accurately and more realistically. There is the example of the *roman expérimental* behind James Joyce, Virginia Woolf, and Dorothy Richardson, and though a little farther removed, behind William Faulkner. But there is a difference, and it is a tremendous one, between Zola and Dreiser, say, two novelists who attempted a kind of laboratory method in fiction, and the stream-of-consciousness writers. It is indicated chiefly in the difference in subject matter—which is, for the earlier novelists, motive and action (external man) and for the later ones, psychic existence and functioning (internal man). The difference is also revealed in the psychological and philosophical thinking in back of this. Psychologically it is the distinction between behavioristic concepts and psychoanalytical ones; philosophically, it is that between a broad materialism and a generalized existentialism. Combined, it is the difference between being concerned about what one does and being concerned about what one is.

I do not offer a Freudian or Existential brief for stream-of-consciousness literature. All of its authors doubtless were familiar, more or less, with psychoanalytical theories and with the twentieth-century recrudescence of personalism and were directly or indirectly influenced by them. Even more certain can we be that these writers were influenced by the broader concepts of a "new psychology" and a "new philosophy"—a nebulous label for all postbehavioristic and nonpositivistic thinking, including any philosophy or psychology which emphasized man's inner mental and emotional life (e.g., Gestalt psychology, psychoanalytical psychology, Bergsonian ideas of *durée* and the *élan vital*, religious mysticism, much symbolic logic, Christian existentialism, etc.). It is this background which led to the great difference between Zola's subject matter and Joyce's; between Balzac's and Dorothy Richardson's. Yet as novelists all of these writers were concerned with the problem of characterization. There is naturalism in character depiction found in the work of both the late and the early of the above novelists, but there is a contrast and it is determined by the difference in psychological focusing. In short, the stream-of-consciousness novelists were, like the naturalists, trying to depict life accurately; but unlike the naturalists, the life they were concerned with was the individual's psychic life.

In examining the chief stream-of-consciousness writers in order to discover their diverse evalutions of inner awareness, we need to keep in mind two important questions: What can be accomplished by presenting character as it exists psychically? How is fictional art enriched by the depiction of inner states? The direction of the following discussion will be toward answering these questions.

Impressions and Visions

Unlike most originators of artistic genres, the twentieth-century pioneer in stream of consciousness remains the least well-known of the important stream-of-consciousness writers. It is the price a writer pays, even an experimental writer, for engendering monotony. Readers may justifiably neglect Dorothy Richardson, but no one who would understand the development of twentieth-century fiction can. With a great debt to Henry James and Joseph Conrad, she invented the fictional depiction of the flow of consciousness. Sometimes she is brilliant; always she is sensitive to the subtleties of mental functioning; but finally, she becomes lost in the overflow—a formless, unending deluge of realistic detail.

It is difficult to grasp Dorothy Richardson's aims. She gives this account of them herself in the brilliant foreword to *Pilgrimage:*

> . . . the present writer, proposing at this moment to write a novel and looking around for a contemporary pattern, was faced with the choice between following one of her regiments and attempting to produce a feminine equivalent of the current masculine realism. Choosing the latter alternative, she presently set aside, at the bidding of a dissatisfaction that revealed its nature without cause, a considerable mass of manuscript. Aware, as she wrote, of the gradual falling away of the preoccupations that for a while had dictated the briskly moving script, and of the substitution, for these inspiring preoccupations, *of a stranger in the form of contemplated reality having for the first time in her experience its own say, and apparently justifying those who acclaim writing as the surest means of discovering the truth about one's own thoughts* and beliefs, she had been at the same time increasingly tormented, not only by the failure, of this now so independently assertive reality, adequately to appear within the text, but by its revelation, whencesoever focused, of a hundred faces, any one of which, the moment it was entrapped within the close mesh of direct statement, summoned its fellows to disqualify it.

The italics are mine and the words they emphasize reveal just what a reader gets from *Pilgrimage.* It is a psychical autobiography, which means that it is almost impossible for a reader to be empathic toward it or to understand the importance of its implications. It is difficult to see either a microcosm or an exemplum here. There is a certain amount of universal interest possible in looking in on how a fairly sensitive but greatly limited mind functions and in discovering how it classifies and rejects; and there is even an interest in discovering what a great amount of dullness a mind encounters in the world—but such an interest is not likely to last throughout twelve volumes. The one possibility left for Dorothy Richardson was to reveal some of the mysteries of psychic life, to depict it as an area from which something of the external world could be explained. But this she does not do. She does not investigate the world of consciousness on a level that is deep enough.

Two interpretations of *Pilgrimage* have suggested a thematic significance in the work: John Cowper Powys, Dorothy Richardson's most persuasive admirer, justifies her novel because it is a presentation of the feminine view of life, which he is convinced is a worth-while thing in itself, necessary to supplement the masculine picture of things. Dorothy Richardson herself evidently believed this also. She says, we recall, that she began writing in order "to produce a feminine equivalent of the current masculine realism." Unfortunately, the dichotomy between the feminine and masculine viewpoints is too tenuous, if not wholly inadequate, for any degree of profundity. Granted a possible overall difference between these two classes of attitudes, still the basic problems and situations of life (hence of art) are neither masculine nor feminine, but simply human. One might as well propose that Faulkner writes in order to present a psychotic equivalent of the current sane realism! Faulkner has, certainly, advantages, which we shall consider presently, in presenting life from an abnormal person's point of view—and likewise there are certain values inherent in the presentation of life from a feminine point of view—but these values cannot be realized in a vacuum.

73

An adequate purpose is not found in presenting these view-points merely for the sake of novelty. It is hardly justified, at least, for important literature. Another critic, Joseph Warren Beach, thinks of *Pilgrimage* as a quest story. He believes the point of the novel lies in Miriam's continuous search for a symbolic "little coloured garden," and again that she is on a pilgrimage "to some elusive shrine, glimpsed here and there and lost to view." This theory is easily credible, and it gives an important justification to the novel; but as Beach intimates, how digressive, how vague, and how long!

Dorothy Richardson deserves more credit as a pioneer in novelistic method than as a successful creator of fiction. There are indications that the pioneering fever was the conscious impetus, for the opening chapters of *Pilgrimage* were "written to the accompaniment of a sense of being upon a fresh pathway, an adventure so searching and, sometimes, so joyous as to produce a longing for participation." By "participation" Dorothy Richardson meant "readers"; but I suspect she will always be rather bland hors d'oeuvres for the reading public. However, another kind of participation came. Dorothy Richardson recognizes this, too, in her foreword: "The lonely track, meanwhile, had turned out to be a populous highway. Amongst those who had simultaneously entered it, two figures stood out. One a woman mounted upon a magnificently caparisoned charger, the other a man walking, with eyes devoutly closed, weaving as he went a rich garment of new words wherewith to clothe the antique dark material of his engrossment." The woman we take to be Virginia Woolf; the man, who is described more aptly, is certainly James Joyce. There is little difficulty in determining why either of these writers used stream-of-consciousness methods.

Virginia Woolf speaks eloquently as a critic herself, and the key to her purposes is in her critical writing. Less eloquently, though authoritatively, are her purposes spoken by a number of other critics, partly because she gives them the key and partly because she lucidly reveals in her novels what she is about. Since Virginia Woolf's accomplishments have been so thoroughly analyzed, it is necessary here only to summarize in order to provide a direct answer to the question which is in front of us: For what purpose does this writer use stream of consciousness?

Let us answer the question at once and show afterward why we have come to the answer. Virginia Woolf wanted to formulate the possibilities and processes of inner realization of truth— a truth she reckoned to be inexpressible; hence only on a level of the mind that is not expressed could she find this process of realization functioning. At least this is true with her three stream-of-consciousness novels. The first two of these, *Mrs. Dalloway* and *To the Lighthouse,* can be considered together, since they illustrate in only slightly different ways the same achievement. *The Waves* marks a different approach.

Clarissa Dalloway, Mrs. Ramsay, and Lily Briscoe all have moments of vision. Not that they are disciplined mystics who have prepared themselves for this, but their creator believed that the important thing in human life is the search the individual constantly has for meaning and identification. The fulfillment of her characters is therefore achieved when Virginia Woolf feels they are ready to receive the vision. The novels are a record of their preparations for the final insight. The preparations are in the form of fleeting insights into other characters and syntheses of present and past private symbols.

We know from Virginia Woolf's essays that she believed the important thing for the artist to express is his private vision of reality, of what life, subjectively, is. She thought that the search for reality is not a matter of dramatic external action. "Examine an ordinary mind on an ordinary day," she says, and again: "Life is . . . a luminous halo, a semi-transparent envelope surrounding us from the beginning of consciousness to the end. Is it not the task of the novelists to convey this varying, this unknown and uncircumscribed spirit . . . ?" Thus the search, thought Virginia Woolf, is a psychic activity, and it is the preoccupation (it surrounds us) of most human beings. The only thing is that most human beings are not aware of this psychic activity, so deep down is it in their consciousness. This is one of the reasons Virginia Woolf chose characters who are extraordinarily sensitive, whose psyches would at least occasionally be occupied with this search. And it is, above all, the reason that she chose the stream-of-consciousness medium for her most mature presentation of this theme.

Analogically, we may call the Virignia Woolf of these two stream-of-consciousness novels a mystic. She is a mystic in that she is interested in the search her characters make for unification. The climax of *Mrs. Dalloway* suggests the mystic's search for cosmic identification. And what, in the novel, is more nearly the mystic's vision of light than Lily Briscoe's crucial attainment of vision in *To the Lighthouse?* It is because this novelist is building up to the moments of illumination that her method is one of presenting psychic impressions. She selects these impressions as stages toward arriving at a vision. It is not the undifferentiated trivia that impinge on consciousness which interest her; it is the illusive event that is meaningful and that carries the germ of the final insight.

The Waves is a different kind of accomplishment. In this novel there is no mystical quest after identity and subjective essence; it is a presentation of the purest psychological analysis in literature. Not, let it be noted, of psychoanalysis. Spontaneous psychic life is presented in this novel. The achievement is the tracing of the growth of psychic lives. The method is as much the presentation of uncensored observations by the characters of each other as it is of the characters' own psychological make-up. Indeed, the two are the same thing in this "X-ray of intuition," as Bernard Blackstone labels it.

The psychic anatomy here is not a bare analysis, however. It is full of the impressionist's sensitivity to color, sound, and shapes as Virginia Woolf's earlier novels are. The formal soliloquies are close to poetry in their concentrated quality, their dependence on rhythms, and their exact diction. This work is the most eloquent of this eloquent novelist's fiction. It is also the most uncommunicative, for here Virginia Woolf's private sense of the significant is confined to characters who remain only individuals and never compose into universal symbols. Reality is the aim and it is achieved, but the rich symbolic significance of the characters of the two earlier stream-of-consciousness novels is lacking. As much as we may admire and enjoy this work, we are almost bound to agree with David Daiches that it is overloaded with technique.

Satires and Ironies

A person much more often charged with such artistic trammeling is James Joyce. In creative productions the ends justify the means, and Joyce has contributed hugely to a revitalized fiction. What the ends of *Ulysses* finally are, I do not expect to determine. The many volumes which have been written to explain Joyce's purposes threaten the cursory appraisal; but I should like at least to suggest one important achievement of Joyce's in *Ulysses* which is central to his whole purpose and which is greatly dependent on stream-of-consciousness techniques. This is the marvelous degree of objectivity which he achieves. Joyce, more than any other novelist, gains what Joseph Warren Beach terms "dramatic immediacy." In *A Portrait of the Artist as a Young Man,* Joyce, in the guise of Stephen, states his theory of the evolution of artistic form when he maintains that "the personality of the artist, at first a cry or a cadence or a mood and then a fluid and lambent narrative, finally refines itself out of existence, impersonalizes itself, so to speak. The esthetic image in the dramatic form is life purified in and projected from the human imagination. The mystery of esthetic like that of material creation is accomplished. The artist, like the God of the creation, remains within or behind or beyond or above his handiwork, invisible, refined out of existence, indifferent, paring his fingernails." The author is almost "refined out of existence" in *Ulysses*. Why does Joyce place such an important emphasis on ridding his work of signs of its author? As a feat in itself it would be nothing more than an interesting tour de force. The effect of this great accomplishment is to make the reader feel he is in direct contact with the life represented in the book. It is a method for doing what Joyce wanted to do, and that is to present life as it actually is, without prejudice or direct evaluations. It is, then, the goal of the realist and the naturalist. The thoughts and actions of the characters are there, as if they were created by an invisible, indifferent creator. We must accept them, because they exist.

If Joyce's accomplishment is, then, that of the most successful of realists, what is his aim? What view of life can he communicate by impersonalizing his creation through presenting the direct interior monologues of his characters? The answer is this—and it is from this basis that a future evaluation of *Ulysses* must start: for Joyce, existence is a comedy and man is to be satirized, gently not bitterly, for his incongruous and pitiful central role in it. The objective distance of the author, working as it chiefly does in *Ulysses* on the level of man's daydreams and mental delusions, shows the smallness of man, the great disparity between his ideals and his actualities, and the prosaicness of most of the things he considers special. Joyce's methods point to this: the *Odyssey* pattern is a means for equating the heroic and the ordinary, and the undifferentiated internal monologue is a means for equating the trivial and the profound. Life is depicted by Joyce so minutely that there is no room for any values to stand out. Joyce presents life with its shortcomings and its inherent contradictions, and the result is satire. Only within stream of consciousness could the necessary objectivity be attained for making it all convincingly realistic; for the pathos is in the fact that *man* thinks he is special and heroic, not that *Joyce* thinks he is pitiful.

Joyce is a writer of comedy and of satiric comedy at that. He is not a jokester or a funny man. The novel is not as a whole, in any sense, a hoax: the overtones are too far-reaching; there is too credible a concept of man's psychic life presented. It is obvious, however, that *Ulysses* is, fundamentally, a satirical comment on modern man's life. Joyce could never have shown this convincingly with any subject other than man's life on the level of consciousness, where the ideal can be reached for, even by the everyman Leopold Bloom, whose very next act or thought will show how far he actually is from it.

The only other writer who utilizes effectively this natural advantage for satire in depiction of psyche is William Faulkner. But there is a difference. Faulkner, although he makes wide use of comic materials, is not a writer of comedy, not even of divine comedy. Faulkner's satires of circumstance are, like those of the Hardy of *Jude the Obscure* and the poems, irrevocably tragic. And they are more profound than Joyce's. One way to explain this is to consider Faulkner as a stream-of-consciousness writer who combines the views of life of Woolf with those of Joyce. Faulkner's views are not the same in either case; but the cast is similar in both. His characters search for insight, and their search is fundamentally ironic.

Since relatively little study has been published on Faulkner, it is necessary to consider his accomplishments more thoroughly than we have those of the other writers. It is tempting to go afield in doing this, but we shall try to focus on answering that question which underlies the present study: Why does Faulkner choose to deal with psychic processes in *The Sound and the Fury* and *As I Lay Dying*? One commentator has it that Faulkner, in the former novel, which we shall consider first, was trying to depict the Freudian idea of dream mechanism and consequently was dealing with unconscious manifestations of libido activity. This certainly, if valid, would automatically put the novel in the stream-of-consciousness genre—if, that is, it could produce a work of art at all. Another writer decides that since the date of the Benjy episode is an Easter Sunday, Benjy is a Christ symbol, etc., which puts the novel I don't know where. These interpretations may be discarded because they involve the heresies of dehumanization, which Faulkner must hate more than anything else. Three much more convincing and sensible critics agree on the basic proposition that all of Faulkner's work can be interpreted on a basis of broad myth and related symbolism. The principle of this interpretation is that Faulkner's entire work is a dramatization, in terms of myth, of the social conflict between the sense of ethical responsibilities in traditional humanism and the amorality of modern naturalism (animalism) in Faulkner, in the South, and by extension, I suppose, universally.

If we begin with this principle as a basis for interpretation of *The Sound and the Fury,* we can understand that the novel is another chapter in the history of the collapse of the humanism of the Sartoris (here Compson) family in a world of the animalism of the Snopeses. The chief character symbol of the Sartoris-Compson code is Quentin III, who commits suicide; the symbol of the Snopes code is Jason IV (actually a Sartoris-Compson), who collapses most completely in that he embraces Snopesism. The other characters represent symbolically stages in degeneracy of, and escape from, the Sartoris-Compson code: Benjy by inherited idiocy; Candace by sexual promiscuity; Mr. Compson by rhetoric and liquor; Mrs. Compson by invalidism; Maury by liquor and laziness. The main conflict then is focused on Quentin and Jason, protagonists respectively of Sections II and III of the novel. But Section I has Benjy as the center of things. The reason for this is that Benjy, with an idiot's mind, is able to present the necessary exposition in not only its simplest tragic terms, but also in terms of symbols, which because they are from an idiot's mind are conveniently general in their meaning and are therefore flexible. It must be remembered, too, that Faulkner saw idiocy as a possible way for a Sartoris-Compson to escape the ethical rigor of a code that depends on exertion of intellect and will. Benjy's role, then, is both to reflect an aspect of Compson degeneracy and to introduce the terms of the main conflict with the simple, forceful symbols available to an idiot.

This conflict is centered on Quentin. Thus the central episode of the novel, which concerns him, is the crucial one. Quentin is determined to preserve the Sartoris-Compson traditions of humanism—in terms of the honor of the Compsons. His obsession is with his sister Candace, who has given in to Snopesism sexually; but Quentin must not accept the fact of her promiscuity, for to him, her honor is a symbol of the dying honor of the Compsons. He convinces himself that he is the violator of Candace's chastity. This conviction is finally without effect because no one else believes him. Eventually Quentin has to accept his defeat and recognition of the Compson defeat. Unable to stand this, he, too, escapes—by suicide.

Faulkner's method puts the struggle in terms of Quentin's psychic conflict, for it is on a prespeech level of mental life that his actual defeat comes—his consciousness defeats him. He can escape everything (he goes to Harvard and he is a gentleman) except his knowledge of the truth. He even attempts to escape his consciousness of the factual world (he takes the hands off his watch; he attempts a substitute for his sister with the little Italian girl), but the only way to do this is by death. In an important sense, then, it is Quentin's consciousness that is his antagonist.

It is almost enough to submit that the advantages of the stream-of-consciousness method for this novel are explained by the central role consciousness itself plays in it. However, we might suggest here the advantages stream-of-consciousness fiction has in presenting symbols as substitutes for rationally formulated ideas. This can be illustrated in both the Benjy and Quentin sections of the novel. The two kinds of mental aberration represented reveal themselves naturally in terms of images and symbols. Because they are represented as coming directly from a premeditative stage of conscious activity, they carry a convincingness and a fuller impact than they otherwise would. The three symbols that signify everything for Benjy (firelight, the pasture, and Candace) are used so frequently that they come to dominate not only Benjy's consciousness, but the reader's also. Yet, such repetition has a naturalness about it because it comes from a mind as simple as Benjy's is. With Quentin, mental simplicity is not the thing; but obsession tends to give the same effect. Here the significance of the odor-of-honeysuckle image, the wedding announcement symbol, and all of the other symbol or image motifs grows in importance simply by the frequent repetition, which repetition is quite natural to an obsessed mind.

On a more immediate basis, the use of stream-of-consciousness techniques is appropriate in this novel because of the fundamental problem involved in describing an idiot or an obsessed person with any objectivity. Faulkner, among others, has done it out of a stream-of-consciousness context (in *The Hamlet, Wild Palms,* etc.), but never has he been able to get the objective distance necessary to prevent either a bizarre or farcical marring of it except in his stream-of-consciousness novels.

An additional effect Faulkner achieves is a contrast in *not* using stream-of-consciousness techniques in the last two episodes of the novel. It is in these sections that Jason's side of the story is presented. The techniques are soliloquy and conventional omniscient narration, with little attempt to present unspoken thoughts. The meaning this change of technique carries is that Jason's acceptance of the amoral Snopesian world is complete—it pervades his whole mental life; hence on the level of psychic life with which the novel had been dealing, there is no conflict for Jason. His conflicts are entirely in the material world of things and acts, not in the ideal one of thoughts.

So, it would seem on first consideration, are those of the characters in Faulkner's other stream-of-consciousness novel, *As I Lay Dying*. The poverty stricken, ignorant, hill folk presented there are, however, not Snopeses, despite their Snopes-like qualities of hypocrisy, promiscuity, and avarice. The macabre pilgrimage to bury the dead, which is the central subject of the novel, is motivated by a sense of duty and honor as rigid as any the Sartoris-Compsons might have.

As I Lay Dying is, then, a marginal work in the Faulkner canon. It functions in relation to the whole Snopes-Sartoris drama as a device for repetition on a lighter scale—a minor parallel theme, so to speak. It deals with neither Snopeses nor Sartorises, but it does deal with the question of ethical codes. The method of presentation involves showing the contrast of the Snopes-like external lives of the Bundrens (the selfishness of Anse, the promiscuity of Dewey Dell, etc.) with the Sartoris-like rigidity of their internal sense of form and moral obligation (the fortitude of Addie, the persistence in duty in Cash, the heroism and loyalty of Jewel, etc.). Through the use of soliloquy to present stream of consciousness, this inner aspect of these hill people is eloquently established. Their humanism is primitive and distorted, but it is as rigid and moral as that of the Sartoris clan; and their animalism is as ugly and perverse as is that of the Snopeses—but there is ignorance, not amorality, at the base.

Stream-of-consciousness fiction is essentially a technical feat. Its successful working-out depended on technical resources exceeding those of any other type of fiction. Because this is so, any study of the genre must be essentially an examination of method. A study of devices and form becomes significant if we understand the achievement that justifies all of the virtuosity. Stream of consciousness is not technique for its own sake. It is based on a realization of the force of the drama that takes place in the minds of human beings.

One writer saw it as metaphysically significant, and her own predilections for the reality of visions led her to demonstrate the insight which the ordinary mind is capable of. For Virginia Woolf, the fleeting but vital visions of the human mind had to be expressed within the setting of that mind—and she was right; for she alone has been able to communicate precisely that sense of vision. Another writer saw it as high comedy, and he saw that it was pitiful too. Joyce's insight into man's mind was complemented by an equal insight into man's surface actions. The juxtaposition of the two was material for comedy, because the comparison between man's aspirations and his achievements was for Joyce the stuff of the comic: incongruity so great it could not produce tears, and if one were as faithless as Joyce was, it could not produce visions either. Faulkner saw one aspect of the drama as a tragedy of blood. (In other aspects he saw it as comedy, both high and low.) "The mind, mind has mountains," Faulkner might say; and he would have to add that the human being usually falls from the sheer cliffs to destruction. The tragedy of being conscious of a dying way of life, and the abortive attempts of the mind to. lead the individual to isolation from the materials of a decaying reality gave Faulkner his themes. These come to the reader most forcibly in that writer's stream-of-consciousness novels, where the scene can be the one in which the tragedy actually takes place.

What these writers have contributed to fiction is broadly one thing: they have opened up for it a new area of life. They have added mental functioning and psychic existence to the already established domain of motive and action. They have created a fiction centered on the core of human experience, which if it has not been the usual domain of fiction, is not, they have proved, an improper one. Perhaps the most significant thing the stream-of-consciousness writers have demonstrated about the mind has been done obliquely: they have, through their contributions, proved that the human mind, especially the artist's, is too complex and wayward ever to be channeled into conventional patterns.

6

Technique as Discovery

BY MARK SCHORER

Modern criticism, through its exacting scrutiny of literary texts, has demonstrated with finality that in art beauty and truth are indivisible and one. The Keatsian overtones of these terms are mitigated and an old dilemma solved if for beauty we substitute form, and for truth, content. We may, without risk of loss, narrow them even more, and speak of technique and subject matter. Modern criticism has shown us that to speak of content as such is not to speak of art at all, but of experience; and that it is only when we speak of the *achieved* content, the form, the work of art as a work of art, that we speak as critics. The difference between content, or experience, and achieved content, or art, is technique.

When we speak of technique, then, we speak of nearly every thing. For technique is the means by which the writer's experience, which is his subject matter, compels him to attend to it; technique is the only means he has of discovering, exploring, developing his subject, of conveying its meaning, and, finally, of evaluating it. And surely it follows that certain techniques are sharper tools than others, and will discover more; that the writer capable of the most exacting technical scrutiny of his subject matter will produce works with the most satisfying content, works with thickness and resonance, works which reverberate, works with maximum meaning.

We are no longer able to regard as seriously intended criticism of poetry which does not assume these generalizations; but the case for fiction has not yet been established. The novel is still read as though its content has some value in itself, as though the subject matter of fiction has greater or lesser value in itself, and as though technique were not a primary but a supplementary element, capable perhaps of not unattractive embellishments upon the surface of the subject, but hardly of its essence. Or technique is thought of in blunter terms than those which one associates with poetry, as such relatively obvious matters as the arrangement of events to create plot; or, within plot, of suspense and climax; or as the means of revealing character motivation, relationship, and development; or as the use of point of view, but point of view as some nearly arbitrary device for the heightening of dramatic interest through the narrowing or broadening of perspective upon the material, rather than as a means toward the positive definition of theme. As for the resources of language, these, somehow, we almost never think of as a part of the technique of fiction—language as used to create a certain texture and tone which in themselves state and define themes and meanings; or language, the counters of our ordinary speech, as forced, through conscious manipulation, into all those larger meanings which our ordinary speech almost never intends. Technique in fiction, all this is a way of saying, we somehow continue to regard as merely a means to organizing material which is "given" rather than as the means of exploring and defining the values in an area of experience which, for the first time *then,* are being given.

Is fiction still regarded in this odd, divided way because it is really less tractable before the critical suppositions which now seem inevitable to poetry? Let us look at some examples: two well-known novels of the past, both by writers who may be described as "primitive," although their relative innocence of technique is of a different sort—Defoe's *Moll Flanders* and Emily Brontë's *Wuthering Heights*; and three well-known novels of this century—*Tono Bungay,* by a writer who claimed to eschew technique; *Sons and Lovers,* by a novelist who, because his ideal of subject matter ("the poetry of the immediate present") led him at last into the fallacy of spontaneous and unchangeable composition, in effect eschewed technique; and *A Portrait of the Artist as a Young Man*, by a novelist whose practice made claims for the supremacy of technique beyond those made by anyone in the past or by anyone else in this century.

Technique in fiction is, of course, all those obvious forms of it which are usually taken to be the whole of it, and many others; but for present purposes, let it be thought of in two respects particularly: the uses to which language, as language, is put to express the quality of the experience in question; and the uses of point of view not only as a mode of dramatic delimitation, but more particularly, of thematic definition. Technique is really what T. S Eliot means by "convention": any selection, structure, or distortion, any form or rhythm imposed upon the world of action; by means of which, it should be added, our apprehension of the world of action is enriched or renewed. In this sense, everything is technique which is not the lump of experience itself, and one cannot properly say that a writer has no technique, or that he eschews technique, for, being a writer, he cannot do so. We can speak of good and bad technique, of adequate and inadequate, of technique which serves the novel's purpose, or disserves.

II

In the prefatory remarks to *Moll Flanders*, Defoe tells us that he is not writing fiction at all, but editing the journals of a woman of notorious character, and rather to instruct us in the necessities and the joys of virtue than to please us. We do not, of course, take these professions seriously, since nothing in the conduct of the narrative indicates that virtue is either more necessary or more enjoyable than vice. On the contrary, we discover that Moll turns virtuous only after a life of vice has enabled her to do so with security; yet it is precisely for this reason that Defoe's profession of didactic purpose has interest. For the actual morality which the novel enforces is the morality of any commercial culture, the belief that virtue pays—in worldy goods. It is a morality somewhat less than skin deep, having no relation to motives arising from a sense of good and evil, least of all, of evil-*in*-good, but exclusively from the presence or absence of food, drink, linen, damask, silver, and timepieces. It is the morality of measurement, and without in the least intending it, *Moll Flanders* is our classic revelation of the mercantile mind: the morality of measurement, which Defoe has completely neglected to measure. He fails not only to evaluate this material in his announced way, but to evaluate it at all. His announced purpose is, we admit, a pious humbug, and he meant us to read the book as a series of scandalous events; and thanks to his inexhaustible pleasure in excess and exaggeration, this element in the book continues to amuse us. Long before the book has been finished, however, this element has also become an absurdity; but not half the absurdity as that which Defoe did not intend at all—the notion that Moll could live a rich and full life of crime, and yet, repenting, emerge spotless in the end. The point is, of course, that she has no moral being, nor has the book any moral life. Everything is external. Everything can be weighed, measured, handled, paid for in gold, or expiated by a prison term. To this, the whole texture of the novel testifies—the bolts of goods, the inventories, the itemized accounts, the landlady's bills, the lists, the ledgers—all this, which taken together comprises what we call Defoe's method of circumstantial realism.

He did not come upon that method by any deliberation; it represents precisely his own world of value, the importance of external circumstance to Defoe. The point of view of Moll is indistinguishable from the point of view of her creator. We discover the meaning of the novel (at unnecessary length, without economy, without emphasis, with almost none of the distortions or the advantages of art) in spite of Defoe, not because of him. Thus the book is not the true chronicle of a disreputable female, but the true allegory of an impoverished soul, the author's; not an anatomy of the criminal class, but of the middle class. And we read it as an unintended comic revelation of self and of a social mode. Because he had no adequate resources of technique to separate himself from his material, thereby to discover and to define the meanings of his material, his contribution is not to fiction but to the history of fiction, and to social history.

The situation in *Wuthering Heights* is at once somewhat the same and yet very different. Here, too, the whole novel turns upon itself, but this time to its estimable advantage; here, too, is a revelation of what is perhaps the author's secret world of value, but this time, through what may be an accident of technique, the revelation is meaningfully accomplished. Emily Brontë may merely have stumbled upon the perspectives which define the form and the theme of her book. Whether she knew from the outset, or even at the end, what she was doing, we may doubt; but what she did and did superbly we can see.

We can assume, without at all becoming involved in the author's life but merely from the tone of somnambulistic excess which is generated by the writing itself, that this world of monstrous passion, of dark and gigantic emotional and nervous energy, is for the author, or was in the first place, a world of ideal value; and that the book sets out to persuade us of the moral magnificence of such unmoral passion. We are, I think, expected, in the first place, to take at their own valuation these demonic beings, Heathcliff and Cathy: as special creatures, set apart from the cloddish world about them by their heightened capacity for feeling, set apart, even, from the ordinary objects of human passion as, in their transcendent, sexless relationship, they identify themselves with an uncompromising landscape and cosmic force. Yet this is absurd, as much of the detail that surrounds it ("Other dogs lurked in other recesses") is absurd. The novelist Emily Brontë had to discover these absurdities to the girl Emily; her technique had to evaluate them for what they were, so that we are persuaded that it is not Emily who is mistaken in her estimate of her characters, but they who are mistaken in their estimate of themselves. The theme of the moral magnificence of unmoral passion is an impossible theme to sustain, and what interests us is that it was device—and this time, mere, mechanical device—which taught Emily Brontë—the needs of her temperament to the contrary, all personal longing and reverie to the contrary, perhaps—that this was indeed not at all what her material must mean as art. Technique objectifies.

To lay before us the full character of this passion, to show us how it first comes into being and then comes to dominate the world about it and the life that follows upon it, Emily Brontë gives her material a broad scope in time, lets it, in fact, cut across three generations. And to manage material which is so extensive, she must find a means of narration, points of view, which can encompass that material, and, in her somewhat crude concept of motive, justify its telling. So she chooses a foppish traveler who stumbles into this world of passionate violence, a traveler representing the thin and conventional emotional life of the far world of fashion, who wishes to hear the tale; and for her teller she chooses, almost inevitably, the old family retainer who knows everything, a character as conventional as the other, but this one representing not the conventions of fashion, but the conventions of the humblest moralism.

What has happened is, first, that she has chosen as her narrative perspective those very elements, conventional emotion and conventional morality, which her hero and heroine are meant to transcend with such spectacular magnificence; and second, that she has permitted this perspective to operate throughout a long period of time. And these two elements compel the novelist to see what her unmoral passions come to. Moral magnificence? Not at all; rather, a devastating spectacle of human waste; ashes. For the time of the novel is carried on long enough to show Heathcliff at last an emptied man, burned out by his fever ragings, exhausted and will-less, his passion meaningless at last. And it goes even a little further, to Lockwood, the fop, in the graveyard, sententiously contemplating headstones. Thus in the end the triumph is all on the side of the cloddish world, which survives.

Perhaps not all on that side. For, like Densher at the end of *The Wings of the Dove,* we say, and surely Hareton and the second Cathy say, "We shall never be again as we were!" But there is more point in observing that a certain body of materials, a girl's romantic daydreams, have, through the most conventional devices of fiction, been pushed beyond their inception in fancy to their meanings, their conception as a written book—that they, that is, are not at all as they were.

III

Technique alone objectifies the materials of art; hence technique alone evaluates those materials. This is the axiom which demonstrates itself so devastatingly whenever a writer declares under the urgent sense of the importance of his materials—whether these are autobiography, or social ideas, or personal passions—whenever such a writer declares that he cannot linger with technical refinements. That art will not tolerate such a writer H. G. Wells handsomely proves. His enormous literary energy included no respect for the techniques of his medium, and his medium takes its revenge upon his bumptiousness. "I have never taken any very great pains about writing. I am outside the hierarchy of conscious and deliberate writers altogether. I am the absolute antithesis of Mr. James Joyce. . . . Long ago, living in close conversational proximity to Henry James, Joseph Conrad, and Mr. Ford Madox Hueffer, I escaped from under their immense artistic preoccupations by calling myself a journalist." Precisely. And he escaped—he disappeared—from literature into the annals of an era.

Yet what confidence! "Literature," Wells said, "is not jewelry, it has quite other aims than perfection, and the more one thinks of 'how it is done' the less one gets it done. These critical indulgences lead along a fatal path, away from every natural interest towards a preposterous emptiness of technical effort, a monstrous egotism of artistry, of which the later work of Henry James is the monumental warning. 'It,' the subject, the thing or the thought, has long since disappeared in these amazing works; nothing remains but the way it has been manipulated." Seldom has a literary theorist been so totally wrong; for what we learn as James grows for us and Wells disappears is that without what he calls "manipulation," there *is* no "it," no "subject" in art. There is again only social history.

The virtue of the modern novelist—from James and Conrad down—is not only that he pays so much attention to his medium, but that, when he pays most, he discovers through it a new subject matter, and a greater one. Under the "immense artistic preoccupations" of James and Conrad and Joyce, the form of the novel changed, and with the technical change, analogous changes took place in substance, in point of view, in the whole conception of fiction. And the final lesson of the modern novel is that technique is not the secondary thing that it semed to Wells, some external machination, a mechanical affair, but a deep and primary operation; not only that technique *contains* intellectual and moral implications, but that it *discovers* them. For a writer like Wells, who wished to give us the intellectual and the moral history of our times, the lesson is a hard one; it tells us that the order of intellect and the order of morality do not exist at all, in art, except as they are organized in the order of art.

Wells' ambitions were very large. "Before we have done, we will have all life within the scope of the novel." But that is where life already is, within the scope of the novel; where it needs to be brought is into novels. In Wells we have all the important topics in life, but no good novels. He was not asking too much of art, or asking that it include more than it happily can; he was not asking anything of it—as art, which is all that it can give, and that is everything.

A novel like *Tono Bungay*, generally thought to be Wells' best, is therefore instructive. "I want to tell—*myself*," says George, the hero, "and my impressions of the thing as a whole"—the thing as a whole being the collapse of traditional British institutions in the twentieth century. George "tells himself" in terms of three stages in his life which have rough equivalents in modern British social history, and this is, to be sure, a plan, a framework; but it is the framework of Wells' abstract thinking, not of his craftsmanship, and the primary demand which one makes of such a book as this—that means be discovered whereby the dimensions of the hero contain the experiences he recounts—is never met. The novelist flounders through a series of literary imitations —from an early Dickensian episode, through a kind of Shavian interlude, through a Conradian episode, to a Jules Verne vision at the end. The significant failure is in that end, and in the way that it defeats not only the entire social analysis of the bulk of the novel, but Wells' own ends as a thinker. For at last George finds a purpose in science. "I decided that in power and knowledge lay the salvation of my life; the secret that would fill my need; that to these things I would give myself."

But science, power, and knowledge are summed up at last in a destroyer. As far as one can tell Wells intends no irony, although he may here have come upon the essence of the major irony in modern history. The novel ends in a kind of meditative rhapsody which denies every value that the book had been aiming toward.

For of all the kinds of social waste which Wells has been describing, this is the most inclusive, the final waste. Thus he gives us in the end not a novel, but a hypothesis; not an individual destiny, but a theory of the future; and not his theory of the future, but a nihilistic vision quite opposite from everything that he meant to represent. With a minimum of attention to the virtues of technique, Wells might still not have written a good novel; but he would at any rate have established a point of view and a tone which would have told us what he meant.

To say what one means in art is never easy, and the more intimately one is implicated in one's material, the more difficult it is. If, besides, one commits fiction to a therapeutic function which is to be operative not on the audience but on the author, declaring, as D. H. Lawrence did, that "One sheds one's sicknesses in books, repeats and presents again one's emotions to be master of them," the difficulty is vast. It is an acceptable theory only with the qualification that technique, which objectifies, is under no other circumstances so imperative. For merely to repeat one's emotions, merely to look into one's heart and write, is also merely to repeat the round of emotional bondage. If our books are to be exercises in self-analysis, then technique must—and alone can—take the place of the absent analyst.

Lawrence, in the relatively late Introduction to his *Collected Poems,* made that distinction of the amateur between his "real" poems and his "composed" poems, between the poems which expressed his demon directly and created their own form "willy-nilly," and the poems which, through the hocus-pocus of technique, he spuriously put together and could, if necessary, revise. His belief in a "poetry of the immediate present," poetry in which nothing is fixed, static, or final, where all is shimmeriness and impermanence and vitalistic essence, arose from this mistaken notion of technique. And from this notion, an unsympathetic critic like D. S. Savage can construct a case which shows Lawrence driven "concurrently to the dissolution of personality and the dissolution of art." The argument suggests that Lawrence's early, crucial novel, *Sons and Lovers,* is another example of meanings confused by an impatience with technical resources.

The novel has two themes: the crippling effects of a mother's love on the emotional development of her son; and the "split" between kinds of love, physical and spiritual, which the son develops, the kinds represented by two young women, Clara and Miriam. The two themes should, of course, work together, the second being, actually, the result of the first: this "split" is the "crippling." So one would expect to see the novel developed, and so Lawrence, in his famous letter to Edward Garnett, where he says that Paul is left at the end with the "drift towards death," apparently thought he had developed it. Yet in the last few sentences of the novel, Paul rejects his desire for extinction and turns toward "the faintly humming, glowing town," to life—as nothing in his previous history persuades us that he could unfalteringly do.

The discrepancy suggests that the book may reveal certain confusions between intention and performance.

One of these is the contradiction between Lawrence's explicit characterizations of the mother and father and his tonal evaluations of them. It is a problem not only of style (of the contradiction between expressed moral epithets and the more general texture of the prose which applies to them) but of point of view. Morel and Lawrence are never separated, which is a way of saying that Lawrence maintains for himself in this book the confused attitude of his character. The mother is a "proud, *honorable* soul," but the father has a "small, *mean* head." This is the sustained contrast; the epithets are characteristic of the whole, and they represent half of Lawrence's feelings. But what is the other half? Which of these characters is given his real sympathy—the hard, self-righteous, aggressive, demanding mother who comes through to us, or the simple, direct, gentle, downright, fumbling, ruined father? There are two attitudes here. Lawrence (and Morel) loves his mother, but he also hates her for compelling his love; and he hates his father with the true Freudian jealousy, but he also loves him for what he is in himself, and he sympathizes more deeply with him because his wholeness has been destroyed by the mother's domination, just as his, Lawrence-Morel's, has been.

This is a psychological tension which disrupts the form of the novel and obscures its meaning, because neither the contradiction in style nor the confusion in point of view is made to right itself. Lawrence is merely repeating his emotions, and he avoids an austerer technical scrutiny of his material because it would compel him to master them. He would not let the artist be stronger than the man.

The result is that, at the same time that the book condemns the mother, it justifies her; at the same time that it shows Paul's failure, it offers rationalizations which place the failure elsewhere. The handling of the girl, Miriam, if viewed closely, is pathetic in what it signifies for Lawrence, both as man and artist. For Miriam is made the mother's scapegoat, and in a different way from the way that she was in life. The central section of the novel is shot through with alternate statements as to the source of the difficulty: Paul is unable to love Miriam wholly, and Miriam can love only his spirit. These contradictions appear sometimes within single paragraphs, and the point of view is never adequately objectified and sustained to tell us which is true. The material is never seen as material; the writer is caught in it exactly as firmly as he was caught in his experience of it. "That's how women are with me," said Paul. "They want me like mad, but they don't want to belong to me." So he might have said, and believed it; but at the end of the novel, Lawrence is still saying that, and himself believing it.

For the full history of this technical failure, one must read

Sons and Lovers carefully and then learn the history of the manuscript from the book called *D. H. Lawrence: A Personal Record*, by one E. T., who was Miriam in life. The basic situation is clear enough. The first theme—the crippling effects of the mother's love—is developed right through to the end; and then suddenly, in the last few sentences, turns on itself, and Paul gives himself to life, not death. But all the way through, the insidious rationalizations of the second theme have crept in to destroy the artistic coherence of the work. A "split" would occur in Paul; but as the split is treated, it is superimposed upon rather than developed in support of the first theme. It is a rationalization made from it. If Miriam is made to insist on spiritual love, the meaning and the power of theme one are reduced; yet Paul's weakness is disguised. Lawrence could not separate the investigating analyst, who must be objective, from Lawrence, the subject of the book; and the sickness was not healed, the emotion not mastered, the novel not perfected. All this, and the character of a whole career, would have been altered if Lawrence had allowed his technique to discover the full meaning of his subject.

A Portrait of the Artist as a Young Man, like *Tono Bungay* and *Sons and Lovers,* is autobiographical, but unlike these it analyzes its material rigorously, and it defines the value and the quality of its experience not by appended comment or moral epithet, but by the texture of the style. The theme of *A Portrait*, a young artist's alienation from his environment, is explored and evaluated through three different styles and methods as Stephen Dedalus moves from childhood through boyhood into maturity. The opening pages are written in something like the Ulyssesean stream of consciousness, as the environment impinges directly on the consciousness of the infant and the child, a strange, opening world which the mind does not yet subject to questioning, selection, or judgment. But this style changes very soon, as the boy begins to explore his surroundings; and as his sensuous experience of the world is enlarged, it takes on heavier and heavier rhythms and a fuller and fuller body of sensuous detail, until it reaches a crescendo of romantic opulence in the emotional climaxes which mark Stephen's rejection of domestic and religious values. Then gradually the style subsides into the austere intellectuality of the final sections, as he defines to himself the outlines of the artistic task which is to usurp his maturity.

A highly self-conscious use of style and method defines the quality of experience in each of these sections, and, it is worth pointing out in connection with the third and concluding section, the style and method evaluate the experience. What has happened to Stephen is, of course, a progressive alienation from the life around him as he progressed in his initiation into it, and by the end of the novel, the alienation is complete. The final portion of the novel, fascinating as it may be for the developing esthetic creed of Stephen-Joyce, is peculiarly bare. The life experience was not bare, as we know from *Stephen Hero*; but Joyce is forcing technique to comment. In essence, Stephen's alienation is a denial of the human environment; it is a loss; and the austere discourse of the final section, abstract and almost wholly without sensuous detail or strong rhythm, tells us of that loss. It is a loss so great that the texture of the notation-like prose here suggests that the end is really all an illusion, that when Stephen tells us and himself that he is going forth to forge in the smithy of his soul the uncreated conscience of his race, we are to infer from the very quality of the icy, abstract void he now inhabits, the implausibility of his aim. For *Ulysses* does not create the conscience of the race; it creates our consciousness.

In the very last two or three paragraphs of the novel, the style changes once more, reverts from the bare, notative kind to the romantic prose of Stephen's adolescence. "Away! Away! The spell of arms and voices: the white arms of roads, their promise of close embraces and the black arms of tall ships that stand against the moon, their tale of distant nations. They are held out to say: We are alone—come." Might one not say that the austere ambition is founded on adolescent longing? That the excessive intellectual severity of one style is the counterpart of the excessive lyric relaxation of the other? And that the final passage of *A Portrait* punctuates the illusory nature of the whole ambition?

For *Ulysses* does not create a conscience. Stephen, in *Ulysses,* is a little older, and gripped now by guilt, but he is still the cold young man divorced from the human no less than the institutional environment. The environment of urban life finds a separate embodiment in the character of Bloom, and Bloom is as lost as Stephen, though touchingly groping for moorings. Each of the two is weakened by his inability to reach out, or to do more than reach out to the other. Here, then, is the theme again, more fully stated, as it were in counterpoint.

But if Stephen is not much older, Joyce is. He is older as an artist not only because he can create and lavish his godlike pity on a Leopold Bloom, but also because he knows now what both Stephen and Bloom mean, and *how much,* through the most brilliant technical operation ever made in fiction, they can be made to mean. Thus *Ulysses,* through the imaginative force which its techniques direct, is like a pattern of concentric circles, with the immediate human situation at its center, this passing on and out to the whole dilemma of modern life, this passing on and out beyond that to a vision of the cosmos, and this to the mythical limits of our experience. If we read *Ulysses* with more satisfaction than any other novel of this century, it is because its author held an attitude toward technique and the technical scrutiny of subject matter which enabled him to order, within a single work and with superb coherence, the greatest amount of our experience.

IV

In the United States during the last twenty-five years, we have had many big novels but few good ones. A writer like James T. Farrell apparently assumes that by endless redundancy in the description of the surface of American life, he will somehow write a book with the scope of *Ulysses*. Thomas Wolfe apparently assumed that by the mere disgorging of the raw material of his experience he would give us at last our epic. But except in a physical sense, these men have hardly written novels at all.

The books of Thomas Wolfe were, of course, journals, and the primary role of his publisher in transforming these journals into the semblance of novels is notorious. For the crucial act of the artist, the unique act which is composition, a sympathetic editorial blue pencil and scissors were substituted. The result has excited many people, especially the young, and the ostensibly critical have observed the prodigal talent with the wish that it might have been controlled. Talent there was, if one means by talent inexhaustible verbal energy, excessive response to personal experience, and a great capacity for auditory imitativeness, yet all of this has nothing to do with the novelistic quality of the written result; for until the talent is controlled, the material organized, the content achieved, there is simply the man and his life. It remains to be demonstrated that Wolfe's conversations were any less interesting as novels than his books, which is to say that his books are without interest as novels. As with Lawrence, our response to the books is determined, not by their qualities as novels, but by our response to him and his qualities as a temperament.

This is another way of saying that Thomas Wolfe never really knew what he was writing *about*. *Of Time and the River* is merely a euphemism for "Of a Man and his Ego." It is possible that had his conception of himself and of art included an adequate respect for technique and the capacity to pursue it, Wolfe would have written a great novel on his true subject—the dilemma of romantic genius; it was his true subject, but it remains his undiscovered subject, it is the subject which *we* must dig out for him, because he himself had neither the lamp nor the pick to find it in and mine it out of the labyrinths of his experience. Like Emily Brontë, Wolfe needed a point of view beyond his own which would separate his material and its effect.

With Farrell, the situation is opposite. He knows quite well what his subject is and what he wishes to tell us about it, but he hardly needs the novel to do so. It is significant that in sheer clumsiness of style no living writer exceeds him, for his prose is asked to perform no service beyond communication of the most rudimentary kind of fact. For his ambitions the style of the newspaper and the lens of the documentary camera would be quite adequate, yet consider the diminution which Leopold Bloom, for example, would suffer, if he were to be viewed from these, the technical perspectives of James Farrell. Under the eye of this technique, the material does not yield up enough; indeed, it shrinks.

More and more writers in this century have felt that naturalism as a method imposes on them strictures which prevent them from exploring through all the resources of technique the full amplifications of their subjects, and that thus it seriously limits the possible breadth of esthetic meaning and response. James Farrell is almost unique in the complacency with which he submits to the blunt techniques of naturalism; and his fiction is correspondingly repetitive and flat.

That naturalism had a sociological and disciplinary value in the nineteenth century is obvious; it enabled the novel to grasp materials and make analyses which had eluded it in the past, and to grasp them boldly; but even then it did not tell us enough of what, in Virginia Woolf's phrase, is "really real," nor did it provide the means to the maximum of reality coherently contained. Even the Flaubertian ideal of objectivity seems, today, an unnecessarily limited view of objectivity, for as almost every good writer of this century shows us, it is quite as possible to be objective about subjective states as it is to be objective about the circumstantial surfaces of life. Dublin, in *Ulysses,* is a moral setting: not only a city portrayed in the naturalistic fashion of Dickens' London, but also a map of the modern psyche with its oblique and baffled purposes. The second level of reality in no way invalidates the first, and a writer like Joyce shows us that, if the artist truly respects his medium, he can be objective about both at once. What we need in fiction is a devoted fidelity to every technique which will help us to discover and to evaluate our subject matter, and more than that, to discover the amplifications of meaning of which our subject matter is capable.

Most modern novelists have felt this demand upon them. André Gide allowed one of his artist-heroes to make an observation which considerably resembles an observation we have quoted from Wells. "My novel hasn't got a subject . . . Let's say, if you prefer it, it hasn't got *one* subject . . . 'A slice of life,' the naturalist school said. The great defect of that school is that it always cuts its slice in the same direction; in time, lengthwise. Why not in breadth? Or in depth? As for me I should like not to cut at all. Please understand; I should like to put everything into my novel." Wells, with his equally large blob of potential material, did not know how to cut it to the novel's taste; Gide cut, of course—in every possible direction. Gide and others. And those "cuts" are all the new techniques which modern fiction has given us. None, perhaps, is more important than that inheritance from French symbolism which Huxley, in the glittering wake of Gide, called "the musicalization of fiction." Conrad anticipated both when he wrote that the novel "must strenuously aspire to the plasticity of sculpture, to the colour of painting, and to the magic suggestiveness of music—which is the art of arts," and when he said of that early but wonderful piece of symbolist fiction, *The Heart of Darkness,* "It was like another art altogether. That sombre theme had to be given a sinister resonance, a tonality of its own, a continued vibration that, I hoped, would hang in the air and dwell on the ear after the last note had been struck."

The analogy with music, except as a metaphor, is inexact, and except as it points to techniques which fiction can employ as fiction, not very useful to our sense of craftsmanship. It has had an approximate exactness in only one work, Joyce's final effort, an effort unique in literary history, *Finnegans Wake,* and here, of course, those readers willing to make the effort Joyce demands, discovering an inexhaustible wealth and scope, are most forcibly reminded of the primary importance of technique to subject, and of their indivisibility.

The techniques of naturalism inevitably curtail subject and often leave it in its original area, that of undefined social experience. Those of our writers who, stemming from this tradition, yet, at their best, achieve a novelistic definition of social experience—writers like the occasional Sherwood Anderson, William Carlos Williams, the occasional Erskine Caldwell, Nathanael West, and Ira Wolfert in *Tucker's People*—have done so by pressing naturalism far beyond itself, into positively Gothic distortions. The structural machinations of Dos Passos and the lyrical interruptions of Steinbeck are the desperate maneuvers of men committed to a method of whose limitations they despair. They are our symbolists *manqué,* who end as allegorists.

Our most accomplished novels leave no such impressions of desperate and intentional struggle, yet their precise technique and their determination to make their prose work in the service of their subjects have been the measure of their accomplishment. Hemingway's *The Sun Also Rises* and Wescott's *The Pilgrim Hawk* are consummate works of art not because they may be measured by some external, neoclassic notion of form, but because their forms are so exactly equivalent with their subjects, and because the evaluation of their subjects exists in their styles.

Hemingway has recently said that his contribution to younger writers lay in a certain necessary purification of the language; but the claim has doubtful value. The contribution of his prose was to his subject, and the terseness of style for which his early work is justly celebrated is no more valuable, as an end in itself, than the baroque involutedness of Faulkner's prose, or the cold elegance of Wescott's. Hemingway's early subject, the exhaustion of value, was perfectly investigated and invested by his bare style, and in story after story, no meaning at all is to be inferred from the fiction except as the style itself suggests that there is no meaning in life. This style, more than that, was the perfect technical substitute for the conventional commentator; it expresses and it measures that peculiar morality of the stiff lip which Hemingway borrowed from athletes. It is an instructive lesson, furthermore, to observe how the style breaks down when Hemingway moves into the less congenial subject matter of social affirmation: how the style breaks down, the effect of verbal economy as mute suffering is lost, the personality of the writer, no longer protected by the objectification of an adequate technique, begins its offensive intrusion, and the entire structural integrity slackens. Inversely, in the stories and the early novels, the technique was the perfect embodiment of the subject and it gave that subject its astonishing largeness of effect and of meaning.

One should correct Buffon and say that style is the subject. In Wescott's *Pilgrim Hawk*—a novel which bewildered its many friendly critics by the apparent absence of subject—the subject, the story, is again in the style itself. This novel, which is a triumph of the sustained point of view, is only bewildering if we try to make a story out of the narrator's observations upon others; but if we read his observations as oblique and unrecognized observations upon himself the story emerges with perfect coherence, and it reverberates with meaning, is as suited to continuing reflection as the greatest lyrics.

The rewards of such respect for the medium as the early Hemingway and the occasional Wescott have shown may be observed in every good writer we have. The involutions of Faulkner's style are the perfect equivalent of his involved structures, and the two together are the perfect representation of the moral labyrinths he explores, and of the ruined world which his novels repeatedly invoke and in which these labyrinths exist. The cultivated sensuousity of Katherine Anne Porter's style—as of Eudora Welty's and Jean Stafford's—has charm in itself, of course, but no more than with these others does it have esthetic value in itself; its values lie in the subtle means by which sensuous details become symbols, and in the way the symbols provide a network which is the story, and which at the same time provides the writer and us with a refined moral insight by means of which to test it. When we put such writers against a writer like William Saroyan, whose respect is reserved for his own temperament, we are appalled by the stylistic irresponsibility we find in him, and by the almost total absence of theme, or defined subject matter, and the abundance of unwarranted feeling. Such a writer inevitably becomes a sentimentalist because he has no means by which to measure his emotion. Technique, at last, is measure.

These writers, from Defoe to Porter, are of unequal and very different talent, and technique and talent are, of course, after a point, two different things. What Joyce gives us in one direction, Lawrence, for all his imperfections as a technician, gives us in another, even though it is not usually the direction of art. Only in some of his stories and in a few of his poems, where the demands of technique are less sustained and the subject matter is not autobiographical, Lawrence, in a different way from Joyce, comes to the same esthetic fulfillment. Emily Brontë, with what was perhaps her intuitive grasp of the need to establish a tension between her subject matter and her perspective upon it, achieves a similar fulfillment; and, curiously, in the same way and certainly by intuition alone, Hemingway's early work makes a moving splendor from nothingness.

And yet, whatever one must allow to talent and forgive in technique, one risks no generalization in saying that modern fiction at its best has been peculiarly conscious of itself and of its tools. The technique of modern fiction, at once greedy and fastidious, achieves as its subject matter not some singleness, some topic or thesis, but the whole of the modern consciousness. It discovers the complexity of the modern spirit, the difficulty of personal morality, and the fact of evil—all the untractable elements under the surface which a technique of the surface alone cannot approach. It shows us—in Conrad's words, from *Victory*—that we all live in an "age in which we are camped like bewildered travellers in a garish, unrestful hotel," and while it puts its hard light on our environment, it penetrates, with its sharp weapons, the depths of our bewilderment. These are not two things, but only an adequate technique can show them as one. In a realist like Farrell, we have the environment only, which we know from the newspapers; in a subjectivist like Wolfe, we have the bewilderment only, which we record in our own diaries and letters. But the true novelist gives them to us together, and thereby increases the effect of each, and reveals each in its full significance.

Elizabeth Bowen, writing of Lawrence, said of modern fiction, "We want the naturalistic surface, but with a kind of internal burning. In Lawrence every bush burns." But the bush burns brighter in some places than in others, and it burns brightest when a passionate private vision finds its objectification in exacting technical search. If the vision finds no such objectification, as in Wolfe and Saroyan, there is a burning without a bush. In our committed realists, who deny the resources of art for the sake of life, whose technique forgives both innocence and slovenliness— in Defoe and Wells and Farrell—there is a bush but it does not burn. There, at first glance, the bush is only a bush; and then, when we look again, we see that, really, the thing is dead.

III   OPENINGS AND EXTENSIONS

7

Pattern and Rhythm

BY E. M. FORSTER

Now we must consider something which springs mainly out
of the plot, and to which the characters and any other element
present also contribute. For this new aspect there appears to be
no literary word—indeed the more the arts develop the more they
depend on each other for definition. We will borrow from painting first and call it the pattern. Later we will borrow from music
and call it rhythm. Unfortunately both these words are vague—
when people apply rhythm or pattern to literature they are apt
not to say what they mean and not to finish their sentences: it is
"Oh but surely the rhythm . . ." or "Oh but if you call that pattern . . ."

Before I discuss what pattern entails, and what qualities a
reader must bring to its appreciation, I will give two examples
of books with patterns so definite that a pictorial image sums
them up: a book the shape of an hour-glass and a book the shape
of a grand chain in that old-time dance, the Lancers.

Thais, by Anatole France, is the shape of an hour-glass.

There are two chief characters, Paphnuce the ascetic, Thais
the courtesan. Paphnuce lives in the desert, he is saved and happy
when the book starts. Thais leads a life of sin in Alexandria, and
it is his duty to save her. In the central scene of the book they
approach, he succeeds; she goes into a monastery and gains salvation, because she has met him, but he, because he has met her, is
damned. The two characters converge, cross, and recede with
mathematical precision, and part of the pleasure we get from the
book is due to this. Such is the pattern of *Thais*—so simple that

it makes a good starting-point for a difficult survey. It is the same as the story of *Thais,* when events unroll in their time-sequence, and the same as the plot of *Thais,* when we see the two characters bound by their previous actions and taking fatal steps whose consequence they do not see. But whereas the story appeals to our curiosity and the plot to our intelligence, the pattern appeals to our aesthetic sense, it causes us to see the book as a whole. We do not see it as an hour-glass—that is the hard jargon of the lecture room which must never be taken literally at this advanced stage of our inquiry. We just have a pleasure without knowing why, and when the pleasure is past, as it is now, and our minds are left free to explain it, a geometrical simile such as an hour-glass will be found helpful. If it was not for this hour-glass the story, the plot, and the characters of Thais and Paphnuce would none of them exert their full force, they would none of them breathe as they do. 'Pattern,' which seems so rigid, is connected with atmosphere, which seems so fluid.

Now for the book that is shaped like the grand chain: *Roman Pictures* by Percy Lubbock.

Roman Pictures is a social comedy. The narrator is a tourist in Rome; he there meets a kindly and shoddy friend of his, Deering, who rebukes him superciliously for staring at churches and sets him out to explore society. This he does, demurely obedient; one person hands him on to another; café, studio, Vatican and Quirinal purlieus are all reached, until finally, at the extreme end of his career he thinks, in a most aristocratic and dilapidated palazzo, whom should he meet but the second-rate Deering; Deering is his hostess's nephew, but had concealed it owing to some backfire of snobbery. The circle is complete, the original partners have rejoined, and greet one another with mutual confusion which turns to mild laughter.

What is so good in *Roman Pictures* is not the presence of the 'grand chain' pattern—any one can organize a grand chain—but the suitability of the pattern to the author's mood. Lubbock works all through by administering a series of little shocks, and by extending to his characters an elaborate charity which causes them to appear in a rather worse light than if no charity was wasted on them at all. It is the comic atmosphere, but sub-acid, meticulously benign. And at the end we discover to our delight that the atmosphere has been externalized, and that the partners, as they click together in the marchesa's drawing-room, have done the exact thing which the book requires, which it required from the start, and have bound the scattered incidents together with a thread woven out of their own substance.

Thais and *Roman Pictures* provide easy examples of pattern; it is not often that one can compare a book to a pictorial object with any accuracy, though curves, etc., are freely spoken of by critics who do not quite know what they want to say. We can only say (so far) that pattern is an aesthetic aspect of the novel, and that though it may be nourished by anything in the novel—any character, scene, word—it draws most of its nourishment from the plot. We noted, when discussing the plot, that it added to itself the quality of beauty; beauty a little surprised at her own arrival: that upon its neat carpentry there could be seen, by those who cared to see, the figure of the Muse; that Logic, at the moment of finishing its own house, laid the foundation of a new one. Here, here is the point where the aspect called pattern is most closely in touch with its material; here is our starting point. It springs mainly from the plot, accompanies it like a light in the clouds, and remains visible after it has departed. Beauty is sometimes the shape of the book, the book as a whole, the unity, and our examination would be easier if it was always this. But sometimes it is not. When it is not I shall call it rhythm. For the moment we are concerned with pattern only.

Let us examine at some length another book of the rigid type, a book with a unity, and in this sense an easy book, although it is by Henry James. We shall see in it pattern triumphant, and we shall also be able to see the sacrifices an author must make if he wants his pattern and nothing else to triumph.

The Ambassadors, like *Thais,* is the shape of an hour-glass. Strether and Chad, like Paphnuce and Thais, change places, and it is the realization of this that makes the book so satisfying at the close. The plot is elaborate and subtle, and proceeds by action or conversation or meditation through every paragraph. Everything is planned, everything fits; none of the minor characters are just decorative like the talkative Alexandrians at Nicias' banquet; they elaborate on the main theme, they work. The final effect is pre-arranged, dawns gradually on the reader, and is completely successful when it comes. Details of intrigue, of the various missions from America, may be forgotten, but the symmetry they have created is enduring.

Let us trace the growth of this symmetry.

Strether, a sensitive middle-aged American, is commissioned by his old friend, Mrs. Newsome, whom he hopes to marry, to go to Paris and rescue her son Chad, who has gone to the bad in that appropriate city. The Newsomes are sound commercial people, who have made money over manufacturing a small article of domestic utility. Henry James never tells us what the small article is, and in a moment we shall understand why. Wells spits it out in *Tono Bungay,* Meredith reels it out in *Evan Harrington,* Trollope prescribes it freely for Miss Dunstable, but for James to indicate how his characters made their pile—it would not do. The article is somewhat ignoble and ludicrous—that is enough. If you choose to be coarse and daring and visualize it for yourself as, say, a button-hook, you can, but you do so at your own risk: the author remains uninvolved.

Well, whatever it is, Chad Newsome ought to come back and help make it, and Strether undertakes to fetch him. He has to be rescued from a life which is both immoral and unremunerative.

114

Strether is a typical James character—he recurs in nearly all
the books and is an essential part of their construction. He is the
observer who tries to influence the action, and who through his
failure to do so gains extra opportunities for observation. And
the other characters are such as an observer like Strether is capable of observing—through lenses procured from a rather too
first-class oculist. Everything is adjusted to his vision, yet he is not
a quietist—no, that is the strength of the device; he takes us
along with him, we move as well as look on.

When he lands in England (and a landing is an exalted and
enduring experience for James, it is as vital as Newgate for Defoe; poetry and life crowd round a landing): when Strether lands,
though it is only old England, he begins to have doubts of his
mission, which increase when he gets to Paris. For Chad Newsome, far from going to the bad, has improved; he is distinguished, he is so sure of himself that he can be kind and cordial
to the man who has orders to fetch him away; his friends are
exquisite, and as for 'women in the case' whom his mother
anticipated, there is no sign of them whatever. It is Paris that
has enlarged and redeemed him—and how well Strether himself
understands this!

> His greatest uneasiness seemed to peep at him out of the
> possible impression that almost any acceptance of Paris might
> give one's authority away. It hung before him this morning,
> the vast bright Babylon, like some huge iridescent object, a
> jewel brilliant and hard, in which parts were not to be dis-
> criminated nor differences comfortably marked. It twinkled
> and trembled and melted together; and what seemed all sur-
> face one moment seemed all depth the next. It was a place of
> which, unmistakably, Chad was fond; wherefore, if he,
> Strether, should like it too much, what on earth, with such a
> bond, would become of either of them?

Thus, exquisitely and firmly, James sets his atmosphere—Paris

115

irradiates the book from end to end, it is an actor though always unembodied, it is a scale by which human sensibility can be measured, and when we have finished the novel and allow its incidents to blur that we may see the pattern plainer, it is Paris that gleams at the centre of the hour-glass shape—Paris—nothing so crude as good or evil. Strether sees this soon, and sees that Chad realizes it better than he himself can; and when he has reached this stage of initiation the novel takes a turn: there is, after all, a woman in the case; behind Paris, interpreting it for Chad, is the adorable and exalted figure of Mme de Vionnet. It is now impossible for Strether to proceed. All that is noble and refined in life concentrates in Mme de Vionnet and is reinforced by her pathos. She asks him not to take Chad away. He promises—without reluctance, for his own heart has already shown him as much—and he remains in Paris not to fight it but to fight for it.

For the second batch of ambassadors now arrives from the New World. Mrs. Newsome, incensed and puzzled by the unseemly delay, has despatched Chad's sister, his brother-in-law, and Mamie, the girl whom he is supposed to marry. The novel now becomes, within its ordained limits, most amusing. There is a superb set-to between Chad's sister and Mme de Vionnet, while as for Mamie—here is disastrous Mamie, seen as we see all things, through Strether's eyes.

As a child, as a 'bud,' and then again as a flower of expansion, Mamie had bloomed for him, freely, in the almost incessantly open doorways of home; where he remembered her at first very forward, as then very backward—for he had carried on at one period, in Mrs. Newsome's parlours, a course of English literature reinforced by exams and teas—and once more, finally, as very much in advance. But he had kept no great sense of points of contact; it not being in the nature of things at Woollett that the freshest of the buds should find herself in the same basket with the most withered of the winter apples. . . . He none the less felt now, as he sat with the charming girl, the signal growth of a confidence. For she *was* charming, when all was said, and none the less so for the visible habit and practice of freedom and fluency. She was charming, he was aware, in spite of the fact that if he hadn't found her so he would have found her something he should have been in peril of expressing as 'funny.' Yes, she was funny, wonderful Mamie, and without dreaming it; she was bland, she was bridal, with never—that he could make out as yet—a bridegroom to support it; she was handsome and portly, and easy and chatty, soft and sweet and almost disconcertingly reassuring. She was dressed, if we might so far discriminate, less as a young lady than as an old one—had an old one been supposable to Strether as so committed to vanity; the complexities of her hair missed moreover also the looseness of youth; and she had a mature manner of bending a little, as to encourage and reward, while she held neatly in front of her a pair of strikingly polished hands: the combination of all of which kept up about her the glamour of her 'receiving,' placed her again perpetually between the windows and within sound of the ice cream plates, suggested the enumeration of all the names, gregarious specimens of a single type, she was happy to 'meet.'

Mamie! She is another Henry James type; nearly every novel contains a Mamie—Mrs. Gereth in *The Spoils of Poynton* for instance, or Henrietta Stackpole in *The Portrait of a Lady*. He is so good at indicating instantaneously and constantly that a character is second rate, deficient in sensitiveness, abounding in the wrong sort of worldliness; he gives such a character so much vitality that its absurdity is delightful.

So Strether changes sides and loses all hopes of marrying Mrs. Newsome. Paris is winning—and then he catches sight of something new. Is not Chad, as regards any fineness in him, played out? Is not Chad's Paris after all just a place for a spree? This fear is confirmed. He goes for a solitary country walk, and at the end of the day he comes across Chad and Mme de Vionnet. They are in a boat, they pretend not to see him, because their relation is at bottom an ordinary liaison, and they are ashamed. They were hoping for a secret week-end at an inn while their passion survived; for it will not survive, Chad will tire of the exquisite Frenchwoman, she is part of his fling; he will go back to his mother and make the little domestic article and marry Mamie. They know all this, and it is revealed to Strether though they try to hide it; they lie, they are vulgar—even Mme de Vionnet, even her pathos, once so exquisite, is stained with commonness.

It was like a chill in the air to him, it was almost appalling, that a creature so fine could be, by mysterious forces, a creature so exploited. For, at the end of all things, they *were* mysterious; she had but made Chad what he was—so why could she think she had made him infinite? She had made him better, she had made him best, she had made him anything one would; but it came to our friend with supreme queerness that he was none the less only Chad. The work, however admirable, was nevertheless of the strict human order, and in short it was marvellous that the companion of mere earthly joys, of comforts, aberrations—however one classed them—within the common experience, should be so transcendently prized.

She was older for him to-night, visibly less exempt from the touch of time; but she was as much as ever the finest and subtlest creature, the happiest apparition, it had been given him, in all his years, to meet; and yet he could see her there as vulgarly troubled, in very truth, as a maidservant crying for a young man. The only thing was that she judged herself as the maidservant wouldn't; the weakness of which wisdom too, the dishonour of which judgment, seemed but to sink her lower.

So Strether loses them too. As he says: "I have lost everything

—it is my only logic." It is not that they have gone back. It is that he has gone on. The Paris they revealed to him—he could reveal it to them now, if they had eyes to see, for it is something finer than they could ever notice for themselves, and his imagination has more spiritual value than their youth. The pattern of the hour-glass is complete; he and Chad have changed places, with more subtle steps than Thais and Paphnuce, and the light in the clouds proceeds not from the well-lit Alexandria, but from the jewel which "twinkled and trembled and melted together, and what seemed all surface one moment seemed all depth the next."

The beauty that suffuses *The Ambassadors* is the reward due to a fine artist for hard work. James knew exactly what he wanted, he pursued the narrow path of aesthetic duty, and success to the full extent of his possibilities has crowned him. The pattern has woven itself, with modulation and reservations Anatole France will never attain. Woven itself wonderfully. But at what sacrifice!

So enormous is the sacrifice that many readers cannot get interested in James, although they can follow what he says (his difficulty has been much exaggerated), and can appreciate his effects. They cannot grant his premise, which is that most of human life has to disappear before he can do us a novel.

He has, in the first place, a very short list of characters. I have already mentioned two—the observer who tries to influence the action, and the second-rate outsider (to whom, for example, all the brilliant opening of *What Maisie Knew* is entrusted). Then there is the sympathetic foil—very lively and frequently female—in *The Ambassadors*. Maria Gostrey plays this part; there is the wonderful rare heroine, whom Mme de Vionnet approached and who is consummated by Milly in *The Wings of the Dove*; there is sometimes a villain, sometimes a young artist with generous impulses; and that is about all. For so fine a novelist it is a poor show.

In the second place, the characters, besides being few in number, are constructed on very stingy lines. They are incapable of fun, of rapid motion, of carnality, and of nine-tenths of heroism. Their clothes will not take off, the diseases that ravage them are anonymous, like the sources of their income, their servants are noiseless or resemble themselves, no social explanation of the world we know is possible for them, for there are no stupid people in their world, no barriers of language, and no poor. Even their sensations are limited. They can land in Europe and look at works of art and at each other, but that is all. Maimed creatures can alone breathe in Henry James' pages—maimed yet specialized. They remind one of the exquisite deformities who haunted Egyptian art in the reign of Akhenaton—huge heads and tiny legs, but nevertheless charming. In the following reign they disappear.

Now this drastic curtailment, both of the numbers of human beings and of their attributes, is in the interests of the pattern. The longer James worked, the more convinced he grew that a novel should be a whole—not necessarily geometric like *The Ambassadors*, but it should accrete round a single topic, situation, gesture, which should occupy the characters and provide a plot, and should also fasten up the novel on the outside—catch its scattered statements in a net, make them cohere like a planet, and swing through the skies of memory. A pattern must emerge, and anything that emerged from the pattern must be pruned off as wanton distraction. Who so wanton as human beings? Put Tom Jones or Emma or even Mr. Casaubon into a Henry James book, and the book will burn to ashes, whereas we could put them into one another's books and only cause local inflammation. Only a Henry James character will suit, and though they are not dead—certain selected recesses of experience he explores very well—

they are gutted of the common stuff that fills characters in other books, and ourselves. And this castrating is not in the interests of the Kingdom of Heaven, there is no philosophy in the novels, no religion (except an occasional touch of superstition), no prophecy, no benefit for the superhuman at all. It is for the sake of a particular aesthetic effect which is certainly gained, but at this heavy price.

H. G. Wells has been amusing on this point, and perhaps profound. In *Boon*—one of his liveliest works—he had Henry James much upon his mind, and wrote a superb parody of him.

James begins by taking it for granted that a novel is a work of art that must be judged by its oneness. Some one gave him that idea in the beginning of things and he has never found it out. He doesn't find things out. He doesn't even seem to want to find things out. He accepts very readily and then— elaborates. . . . The only living human motives left in his novels are a certain avidity and an entirely superficial curiosity. . . . His people nose out suspicions, hint by hint, link by link. Have you ever known living human beings do that? The thing his novel is *about* is always there. It is like a church lit but with no congregation to distract you, with every light and line focused on the high altar. And on the altar, very reverently placed, intensely there, is a dead kitten, an egg shell, a piece of string. . . . Like his *Altar of the Dead* with nothing to the dead at all. . . . For if there was, they couldn't all be candles, and the effect would vanish.

Wells sent *Boon* as a present to James, apparently thinking the master would be as much pleased by such heartiness and honesty as was he himself. The master was far from pleased, and a most interesting correspondence ensued. Each of the eminent men becomes more and more himself as it proceeds. James is polite, reminiscent, bewildered, and exceedingly formidable: he admits that the parody has not "fiilled him with a fond elation," and

regrets in conclusion that he can sign himself "only yours faithfully, Henry James." Wells is bewildered too, but in a different way; he cannot understand why the man should be upset.
And, beyond the personal comedy, there is the great literary importance of the issue. It is this question of the rigid pattern:
hour-glass or grand chain or converging lines of the cathedral or
diverging lines of the Catherine wheel, or bed of Procrustes—
whatever image you like as long as it implies unity. Can it be
combined with the immense richness of material which life provides? Wells and James would agree it cannot. Wells would go
on to say that life should be given the preference, and must not
be whittled or distended for a pattern's sake. My own prejudices
are with Wells. The James novels are a unique possession and the
reader who cannot accept his premises misses some valuable and
exquisite sensations. But I do not want more of his novels,
especially when they are written by some one else, just as I do
not want the art of Akhenaton to extend into the reign of Tut-
ankhamen.

That then is the disadvantage of a rigid pattern. It may ex-
ternalize the atmosphere, spring naturally from the plot, but it
shuts the doors on life and leaves the novelist doing exercises,
generally in the drawing-room. Beauty has arrived, but in too
tyrannous a guise. In plays—the plays of Racine, for instance—
she may be justified, because beauty can be a great empress on
the stage, and reconcile us to the loss of the men we knew. But
in the novel, her tyranny as it grows powerful grows petty, and
generates regrets which sometimes take the form of books like
Boon. To put it in other words, the novel is not capable of as
much artistic development as the drama: its humanity or the
grossness of its material hinder it (use which ever phrase you like).
To most readers of fiction the sensation from a patern is not
intense enough to justify the sacrifices that made it, and their
verdict is "Beautifully done, but not worth doing."

Still this is not the end of our quest. We will not give up the hope of beauty yet. Cannot it be introduced into fiction by some other method than the pattern? Let us edge rather nervously towards the idea of 'rhythm.'

Rhythm is sometimes quite easy. Beethoven's Fifth Symphony, for instance, starts with the rhythm 'diddidy dum,' which we can all hear and tap to. But the symphony as a whole has also a rhythm—due mainly to the relation between its movements—which some people can hear but no one can tap to. This second sort of rhythm is difficult, and whether it is substantially the same as the first sort only a musician could tell us. What a literary man wants to say though is that the first kind of rhythm, the diddidy dum, can be found in certain novels and may give them beauty. And the other rhythm, the difficult one—the rhythm of the Fifth Symphony as a whole—I cannot quote you any parallels for that in fiction, yet it may be present.

Rhythm in the easy sense is illustrated by the work of Marcel Proust.

Proust's conclusion has not been published yet, and his admirers say that when it comes everything will fall into its place, times past will be recaptured and fixed, we shall have a perfect whole. I do not believe this. The work seems to me a progressive rather than an aesthetic confession, and with the elaboration of Albertine the author was getting tired. Bits of news may await us, but it will be surprising if we have to revise our opinion of the whole book. The book is chaotic, ill constructed, it has and will have no external shape; and yet it hangs together because it is stitched internally, because it contains rhythms.

There are several examples (the photographing of the grandmother is one of them), but the most important, from the binding point of view, is his use of the 'little phrase' in the music of Vinteuil. It does more than anything else—more even than the jealousy which successively destroys Swann, the hero, and Charlus

123

—to make us feel that we are in a homogeneous world. We first hear Vinteuil's name in hideous circumstances. The musician is dead—an obscure little country organist, unknown to fame—and his daughter is defiling his memory. The horrible scene is to radiate in several directions, but it passes, we forget about it.

Then we are at a Paris salon. A violin sonata is performed and a little phrase from its andante catches the ear of Swann and steals into his life. It is always a living being, but takes various forms. For a time it attends his love for Odette. The love affair goes wrong, the phrase is forgotten, we forget it. Then it breaks out again when he is ravaged by jealousy, and now it attends his misery and past happiness at once, without losing its own divine character. Who wrote the sonata? On hearing it is by Vinteuil, Swann says, "I once knew a wretched little organist of that name—it couldn't be by him." But it is, and Vinteuil's daughter and her friend transcribed and published it.

That seems all. The little phrase crosses the book again and again, but as an echo, a memory; we like to encounter it, but it has no binding power. Then, hundreds and hundreds of pages on, when Vinteuil has become a national possession, and there is talk of raising a statue to him in the town where he has been so wretched and so obscure, another work of his is performed—a posthumous sextet. The hero listens—he is in an unknown rather terrible universe while a sinister dawn reddens the sea. Suddenly for him and for the reader too, the little phrase of the sonata recurs—half heard, changed, but giving complete orientation, so that he is back in the country of his childhood with the knowledge that it belongs to the unknown.

We are not obliged to agree with Proust's actual musical descriptions (they are too pictorial for my own taste), but what we must admire is his use of rhythm in literature, and his use of something which is akin by nature to the effect it has to produce —namely a musical phrase. Heard by various people—first by

Swann, then by the hero—the phrase of Vinteuil is not tethered: it is not a banner such as we find George Meredith using—a double-blossomed cherry tree to accompany Clara Middleton, a yacht in smooth waters for Cecilia Halkett. A banner can only reappear, rhythm can develop, and the little phrase has a life of its own, unconnected with the lives of its auditors, as with the life of the man who composed it. It is almost an actor, but not quite, and that 'not quite' means that its power has gone towards stitching Proust's book together from the inside, and towards the establishment of beauty and the ravishing of the reader's memory. There are times when the little phrase—from its gloomy inception, through the sonata, into the sextet—means everything to the reader. There are times when it means nothing and is forgotten, and this seems to me the function of rhythm in fiction; not to be there all the time like a pattern, but by its lovely waxing and waning to fill us with surprise and freshness and hope.

Done badly, rhythm is most boring, it hardens into a symbol and instead of carrying us on it trips us up. With exasperation we find that Galsworthy's spaniel John, or whatever it is, lies under the feet again; and even Meredith's cherry trees and yachts, graceful as they are, only open the windows into poetry. I doubt that it can be achieved by the writers who plan their books beforehand, it has to depend on a local impulse when the right interval is reached. But the effect can be exquisite, it can be obtained without mutilating the characters, and it lessens our need of an external form.

That must suffice on the subject of easy rhythm in fiction: which may be defined as repetition plus variation, and which can be illustrated by examples. Now for the more difficult question. Is there any effect in novels comparable to the effect of the Fifth Symphony as a whole, where, when the orchestra stops, we hear something that has never actually been played? The opening movement, the andante, and the trio-scherzo-trio-finale-trio-finale

125

that composes the third block, all enter the mind at once, and extend one another into a common entity. This common entity, this new thing, is the symphony as a whole, and it has been achieved mainly (though not entirely) by the relation between the three big blocks of sound which the orchestra has been playing. I am calling this relation 'rhythmic.' If the correct musical term is something else, that does not matter; what we have now to ask ourselves is whether there is any analogy to it in fiction.

I cannot find any analogy. Yet there may be one; in music fiction is likely to find its nearest parallel.

The position of the drama is different. The drama may look towards the pictorial arts, it may allow Aristotle to discipline it, for it is not so deeply committed to the claims of human beings. Human beings have their great chance in the novel. They say to the novelist: "Recreate us if you like, but we must come in," and the novelist's problem, as we have seen all along, is to give them a good run and to achieve something else at the same time. Whither shall he turn? not indeed for help but for analogy. Music, though it does not employ human beings, though it is governed by intricate laws, nevertheless does offer in its final expression a type of beauty which fiction might achieve in its own way. Expansion. That is the idea the novelist must cling to. Not completion. Not rounding off but opening out. When the symphony is over we feel that the notes and tunes composing it have been liberated, they have found in the rhythm of the whole their individual freedom. Cannot the novel be like that? Is not there something of it in *War and Peace*?—the book with which we began and in which we must end. Such an untidy book. Yet, as we read it, do not great chords begin to sound behind us, and when we have finished does not every item—even the catalogue of strategies—lead a larger existence than was possible at the time?

8

Myth as Literature

BY RICHARD CHASE

Nearly all of our writers agree that in early times myth and religion are next to indistinguishable and that myth is a kind of religious philosophy. Furthermore, nearly all of our writers tell us that myth was born out of primitive man's fear and adoration of nature or out of his curiosity concerning nature. Those authors who have accepted the degeneration theory of history tell us that myth is or was once an esoteric metaphysical or allegorical philosophy; the evolutionists tell us that myth is a crude, false philosophy. Hume observed that "the vulgar" do not philosophize about the universe and Otfried Müller chose not to study cosmogonic myths because, in his estimation (no doubt an *over*estimation) these represented only 10 per cent of Greek myths. Nevertheless for most of our authors myth was pre-eminently philosophical, and the reader of these pages must often have felt that this preoccupation came more and more to exclude some of the most interesting and fruitful problems of mythology.

One such problem is posed by John Dewey: "Myths," he writes, "were something other than intellectualistic essays of primitive man in science . . . delight in the story . . . played its dominant part then as it does in the growth of popular mythologies today. Not only does the direct sense element . . . tend to absorb all ideational matter but . . . it subdues and digests all that is merely intellectual." Mythology, says Dewey, "is much more an affair of the psychology that generates art than an effort at scientific and philosophical explanation." The American anthropologists agree with Dewey in discounting the philosophical function of myth. Those who stress the importance of exceptional individuals think that the philosophical ideas in mythology were imposed by individual thinkers upon already existing myths of the people, which were simply imaginary tales about human life. They do not deny what the nineteenth-century thinkers insisted upon: that some myths give philosophical explanations of nature, of the origin of the world, of the migrations of sun, moon, and stars. When we look superficially from mythology to mythology these concepts are likely to strike us as the only stable element of myth. But it is a great mistake—the mistake of the comparative method—to assume, because a handful of philosophical concepts and explanations are relatively clearcut and appear in many different mythologies, that these are fundamentally characteristic of myth. A close examination of one culture area (a group of tribes who have exerted cultural influence on one another and who possess certain cultural elements in common) shows that the fundamental myth is the dramatic human tale. It is the philosophical explanations which appear to be unstable when we notice that different tribes may tell the same story but that in one case it is explanatory and in five or six other cases it is not. Even within the same tribe a dramatic tale may be told of a mother, father, uncle, and children who in one version are purely human while in another version they acquire some of the characteristics of the moon, the sun, and the stars. In many such semi-celestial tales there is no philosophizing or explanation but only an aesthetic solicitation of nature by a storyteller of a particular and probably unusual temperament. Boas appears to state the general view of the American anthropologists when he concludes that to interpret the myths which have been collected from the primitive mythmakers themselves "as a reflection of the observation of nature is obviously not justifiable." The Crow Indians will tell you that their Great Being is the Sun. But they are extremely vague and confused as to his characteristics. He is always merging with that much more tangible deity, Old Man Coyote, the Crow culture hero. "The Sun" is an extrusion, a mostly useless rationalization. Is it entirely reasonable to assume that all men, like many nineteenth-century philosophers, are more interested in nature than in themselves?

The older writers now seem to us to have neglected a simple and fundamental truth: *the word "myth" means story: a myth is a tale, a narrative, or a poem; myth is literature and must be considered as an aesthetic creation of the human imagination.* A myth need be no more philosophical than any other kind of literature. In one sense we may say that there is no such thing as *a* myth, but only poetical stories which are more or less mythical; we may, however, call a story or tale which is primarily mythical a "myth" and we may use "story" or "tale" for a narrative which is not primarily mythical.

As soon as we begin to think of myth as literature there are three immediate questions to be answered. Are there any primitive peoples who have myths but no literature? What kinds of literature do primitive peoples have? What are the relations between them?

The answer to the first question is that no people has ever been known to be without a literature. Tales and songs are world-wide, writes Professor Boas. "The Bushman and the Eastern Eskimo, although poor in the production of art, are rich in tales and songs, of which they possess a well-nigh inexhausible treasure. The poor hunter of the Malay peninsula and the Australians have their literature no less than economically more advanced people. Songs and tales are found all over the world. These are the fundamental forms of literature among primitive people." In fairness to the older students of myth we must observe here that the universality of primitive literature had become known only to the relatively recent collectors of folklore, who, following the example of the brothers Grimm, have brought together an overwhelming body of folk literature from both primitive and civilized countries.

The division of Greek mythological literature made by Heyne and Herder has become more or less standard in modern times. Sir James Frazer carries this division to its logical conclusion. *Myths proper,* he writes, are concerned with the origin of the world and man, the motions of the stars, the vicissitudes of vegetation, weather, eclipses, storms, the discovery of fire, the invention of the useful arts, the mystery of death. *Legends* are "traditions, whether oral or written, which relate the fortunes of real people in the past, or which describe events, not necessarily human, that are said to have occurred at real places." *Folk tales* are "purely imaginary, having no other aim than the entertainment of the hearer and making no real claim on his credulity." Frazer refers to the stories of Meleager, Melampus, Medea, Glaucus, Perseus, Peleus, Thetis, and Polyphemus as folk tales. Malinowski makes a similar division in his "Myth in Primitive Psychology," pointing out that he is following a division made by the natives themselves (the Trobriand Islanders).

Some American anthropologists appear to suppose that the literary categories made by certain American Indian tribes as well as by the Greeks and other peoples are generally applicable. Myths, according to this formulation, are tales relating to a past mythological age, when the world was different from its present state. Folk tales are stories of present or of recent events. (To the anthropologists "legends" apparently do not emerge as a clear category, being absorbed into myth or folk tale. It is no doubt true that a certain durability of tradition must obtain before legend can flourish, and tradition in most primitive societies is tenuous.) For our purposes this division is not of much use. In the first place the sense of the pastness of the mythological past seems to be sometimes so vague that another way of describing the emotion involved must be found. The Eskimos have a relatively flourishing mythology; but they have practically no sense of the remote past. To the Eskimo, writes Professor Boas, "the world has always been as it is now." To primitive man the mythological past is an emotion felt and not an epoch conceived. The savage's sense of pastness is closely akin to his general sense of the preternatural world. That the "mythological age" may be something personally experienced, something to which in myth-making one may "regress," is suggested by Lévy-Bruhl, who shows that certain primitive peoples use the same word to signify both "dream" and "the mythical period." If the sense of the past differs qualitatively from the general sense of the preternatural, it is perhaps because it arises from a regression to childhood. But as the psychoanalysts have shown, aesthetic activity is in many complicated ways a matter of regression to one's childhood. In this sense, "the past" surely weaves a complex pattern into all kinds of primitive literature, and it would be highly arbitrary to identify as myths those stories which explicitly refer to the past in such a way that it may be historically conceived.

Furthermore, creatures who seem to belong to "the mythical period" are always appearing in "folk tales." Again, the same tale may be told of the mythological age as is told elsewhere of the present or recent past. It is of course instructive that so many peoples identify their myths as such because they are stories which take place in the mythological age, when the world was different. But we cannot be satisfied with this as a definition. If we accept it as Boas does, we do not find it of much use, nor does Boas, as is demonstrated by his most definitive essay on myth, "Folktales of the North American Indians." Why does the mythmaker as he relates his tale to his audience imagine a time when the world was different? What use does he make of this idea? What needs call it into existence? What emotions does the evocation of the past arouse? These are questions which ask, "What is the function of myth?" And it is the *function* of myth that we must consider in answering all such questions.

Nor do other familiar distinctions between kinds of primitive literature seem ultimately fruitful. For example, the same tale may in different guises be explanatory or nonexplanatory, celestial or terrestrial; and the same tale may vary widely between the natural and the preternatural, or place a widely varying emphasis on the human, animal, spiritual, ghostly, or divine characters. As Professor Boas himself remarks, when a single cultural area, such as the Northwest Coast of America, is subjected to careful analysis, it appears that the folk tales and myths constantly blend into each other. It seems to me that any rigid attempt to distinguish among myth and legend and folk tale is open to so many objections as to be of very limited (though sometimes of very real) utility. What is important is to arrive at a definition of myth which cuts across these uncertain categories. First, however, let us look briefly at three theories of the historical relation between the different kinds of primitive literature.

(1) The Grimm brothers adhered to the degeneration theory which went hand in hand with Indo-European linguistics. The *Märchen* or folk tales were supposed to be remnants of primordial Aryan myths depicting "the mysterious and terrible forces of nature." They were fictitious misreadings of "a belief dating back to the most ancient times" which "can only be discovered by the most far-seeing eye." So Wilhelm Grimm wrote in 1856, three years before he died. But he seems to have had some doubts even as he wrote. He had thought that the *Märchen* "were coterminous with . . . the great race which is commonly called Indo-Germanic"—but "we see with amazement" that similar stories appear among the African Negroes and the American Indians. In an earlier time Sir Walter Scott espoused the degeneration theory: "the mythology of one period," he writes, "would appear

to pass into the romance of the next, and that into the nursery tales of subsequent ages." At a later time Max Müller repeated this argument.

(2) In his later years, Andrew Lang became more and more interested in the folk tale, and the philosophical savage with his scientific myths began to assume a new perspective. Lang did not live to develop a full theory, but his evolutionary habit of mind led him to think that the folk tale, undoubtedly a universal phenomenon, must be anterior to the myth. "Märchen," he wrote, are the "oldest extant form of the higher myths." By "higher myth," he seems to mean legends: thus the stories of Perseus, Odysseus, Jason, Leminkainen, Maui (the Maori culture hero) are composed of earlier *Märchen*, originally told of anonymous people or animals, later localized and attached to a real or imaginary personage. He does not definitely include the myth proper—the "explanatory myth"—in this evolutionary process, contenting himself with a vague but very suggestive reference to "elaborate myths" developed by "poets and priests . . . out of the original savage data." E. S. Hartland, one of Lang's colleagues in the Folklore Society, appears to have given the folk tale general primacy: "modern European folktales," he wrote, "cannot be the worn-down relics of the classical mythology. They are rather stuff of the kind out of which the classical or other mythologies grew." Wilhelm Wundt says that the *Märchen* was "the original narrative," "the most permanent of all forms of literary composition." He believes that it was a product of a universal "totemic age," and even insists on what is undoubtedly true: that the content, at least, of cosmogonic myths corresponds to "Märchen of a very primitive type," though their form and import belong to a much higher stage of development.

(3) The generally accepted view today is that, aside from probable but undemonstrable evolutionary theories, the folk tale is psychologically and functionally primary to the more am-

bitious and serious mythological tales. The tendency is to suppose that obviously philosophical or explanatory myths are tales which have been remodeled and intellectualized by gifted priests or raconteurs. No modern anthropologist would deny, however, that some highly developed myths have in some places been retold and misread in folktale style, and in this sense have degenerated.

With few exceptions, modern anthropologists agree that primitive man, like civilized man, lives in two worlds, the matter-of-fact workaday world and the magico-religious world and that he employs various psychic and social devices for keeping them separate. Primitive man is sometimes rational and practical, sometimes irrational and superstitious. He has two principles of causation: the natural and what may be rather vaguely called the supernatural.

But here a note of definition upon which much of our later argument depends. Whatever may be true of the study of religion, in the study of myth the word "preternatural" has certain advantages over the more common "supernatural." *Super*natural implies a philosophical distinction between the objective and the supersensuous which the savage does not make and which we ought not to make in studying mythopoeic psychology. Furthermore, it has misleading theological overtones. "Preternatural" means, in these pages, *that which is magical, the Uncanny, the Wonderful, the Mysterious, the Powerful, the Terrible, the Dangerous, the Extraordinary. In short, anything that has mana is preternatural.*

Whether or not primitive religion may best be understood by assuming a supernatural world of causes and events as opposed to a natural world, such a dualism appears to be misleading in the study of myth. The preternatural, which is aesthetically apprehended and controlled by myths, does, it is true, set itself off from the real world as we ordinarily perceive it. But that is not because it is *less* than ordinarily real but because it is far *more* than ordinarily real—an idea we shall now try to develop.

Otfried Müller's definition of myth as a narrative which unites the real and the ideal (i.e., the imaginary, not the moral ideal) is basically correct. We prefer to say, however, that myth is literature which suffuses the natural with preternatural efficacy (*mana*). But not all literature which does this is myth. Within our broad definition a myth is to be distinguished from other kinds of literature *by its function*.

In his "Myth in Primitive Psychology" Malinowski had made an admirable statement of the use of myth among the Trobriand Islanders. That mythmaking is not merely a useless and unaccountable pastime or the indulgence of one's curiosity is agreed upon by all modern anthropologists. Malinowski's statement of the functionalism of myth, however, is the most complete and perhaps the most extreme that has been made. He thinks that myth "is a hard-working, extremely important cultural force." It is "a narrative resurrection of a primeval reality, told in satisfaction of deep religious wants, moral craving, social submissions, even practical requirements." It is a pragmatic charter of primitive faith and moral wisdom which "comes into play when rite, ceremony, or a social or moral rule demands justification, warrant of antiquity, reality and sanctity." Finally, it is "a statement of primeval, greater, and more relevant reality by which the present life, fates, and activities of mankind are determined." Although he shows that myth is a strong preservative of tradition, Malinowski denies that it is dogma. It may have the efficacy of dogma, but it is at the same time plastic and dynamic. Myths are made *ad hoc,* he writes; they are "constantly regenerated; every historical change creates its mythology."

If a narrative suffuses the natural with the preternatural in reinforcement of the sanctity, the reality, the worth-whileness of any serious cultural activity of or life itself, may we not say that the narrative is a myth?

Malinowski's account of myth as we have sketched it is confined to the myth proper and does not include the folk tale. According to this account, moreover, the function of myth is primarily moral and social, rather than psychological. Any complete statement of the function of myth would have to bring out more clearly its psychological function and would have to deal with the folk tale rather than dismiss it, as does Malinowski, because it is not "serious."

Much of the time the savage, like everyone else, languishes in apathy and mechanical routine; his emotions, as Dewey writes, are often "sodden." Yet he is perhaps more often capable of a dynamic and precise attention than we are. Goldenweiser writes that primitive culture is "dynamic and vibrant." The tenuousness of the savage's sense of history and tradition is partly compensated for by an exaggerated system of ritual and taboos designed in part to preserve accepted values. Yet his inadequate sense of the past demands a correspondingly rich sense of the present; and his struggles in a precarious economic and a hostile natural environment make a "vibrant" sense of present reality a vital necessity. What is "real" to the savage does not, of course, mean that which is scientifically verifiable. Reality to him (to most of us, for that matter) is that which seems to have power, that which seems to have *mana*. While the need for a sense of reality may not be so pressing to those who live in a complex society which furnishes various kinds of contrived security, to the savage it is often a matter of life and death. When he is thinking and feeling at the height of his powers, he lives, as Radin says, "in a blaze of reality."

If, then, the myth as distinguished from the legend and the folk tale is "a narrative resurrection of a primeval reality," we may perhaps say that myth in general is a resurrection of reality, and that, no less than the serious myths, the folk tale, which constitutes the fundamental corpus of mythology, resurrects the sense of reality by suffusing the objective universe with preternatural force—does so, that is, when it becomes mythical. Marett suggested that myth "need be no more than a sort of animatism grown picturesque." We may translate this by saying that myth is *mana* grown picturesque. The psychological function of countless narratives about ghosts, magical objects, enchanted forests, lost children, malevolent, benign, or irresponsible culture heroes, animals which change into men or become their guardian spirits, cosmological beings, etc., is to fuse the perception of magical power with the perception of color, size, shape, sound, or motion.

"The world of myth," as Professor Ernst Cassirer writes, "is a dramatic world—the world of actions, of forces, of conflicting powers." Now when forces are apprehended as felt qualities they become usable in an art form. But it is not only such qualities as color or sound which to the mythmaker are indistinguishable from the object which excites him. He perceives objects "physiognomically," as Cassirer says; objects change "their usual faces" in accordance with the mythmaker's emotions. Dramatic qualities in naïve experience, according to Dewey, "stand in themselves on precisely the same level as colors, sounds, qualities of contact, taste and smell. . . . Empirically things are poignant, tragic, beautiful, humorous, settled, disturbed, comfortable, annoying, barren, harsh, consoling, splendid, fearful; are such immediately in their own right and in their own behalf." The magician unconsciously assumes the fusion of power, quality, and object. But besides being a compulsive technique magic is in and of itself an aesthetic activity. Magic is immediately available to art, and art to magic. Myths may be regarded, on the one hand, as the aesthetic exercise which preserves and reaffirms the magic fusion; myths keep the magician's world—and the poet's world—from falling apart. On the other hand, myths are poetic dramatizations of the conflicts and interactions of powers operating within the qualities and objects with which these powers seem to be identical. If these observations are sound, any narrative or poem which reaffirms the dynamism and vibrancy of the world, which fortifies the ego with the impression that there is a magically potent brilliancy or dramatic force in the world, may be called a myth.*

Primitive literature may also be said to perform what I venture to call the Promethean task of reconciling the conflicting forces of magic and religion. This idea, however, demands some preliminary remarks.

In his *Natural History of Religion* Hume very cannily chose examples of what we should now call magic to illustrate the myth-making mind at work. Magic is not conducive to a highly developed mythology because it does not of itself postulate spirits or gods or personifications of natural objects and forces. Never-

---

* If we define metaphor as the figurative fusion of two (or more) activities, the present discussion obviously raises the question of the relation between metaphor and myth. Vico thought, as we have seen, that "every metaphor is the abridgement of a fable." This is true if we specify the two active worlds which the metaphor fuses as the preternatural and the natural and then select, among metaphors which do this, those which operate as myth does. We might notice in passing that the practice of magic must have been a powerful influence in conditioning the aesthetic psychology to metaphor and simile. This is because of the endless analogies the magician makes between his own mental and emotive processes and the external activities of the world, and between different objects. As Professor Benedict writes, "practically all the similitudes in nature have been employed somewhere in the magic of some people" (*General Anthropology*, 639).

A symbol may perhaps be described roughly as a precipitated metaphor, as crystals are precipitated out of chemical solutions. Vico was right to insist that myth is not primarily symbolic. He is amply supported in this opinion by modern anthropologists such as B. Malinowski ("Myth in Primitive Psychology," 73) and Radin (*Primitive Man as Philosopher*, 209). Primitive art uses symbols: all art does. But the symbol is something likely to be read by commentators into what was created by the fluid play of the imagination. A pointed interest in the use of symbols is not so characteristic of savages as it is of semanticists.

theless the whole groundwork of myth is magical; for the story-teller can compose myths about wonderfully potent animals and men who defy the laws of time and space, as well as the laws which limit the mutability of species, and still remain close to the confines of the psychology of magic. Magic, of course, emphasizes the power of men as opposed to the power of gods, and what interested Hume, and Herbert Spencer, was precisely the limitations which men place upon their gods. Even in highly developed mythologies we find the attitude of the magician. There are countless stories not only of the positive compulsion of gods but of gods being beaten, cajoled, bribed, tricked, scolded, and insulted. This treatment of the gods is but one aspect of the pervasive desire of the storyteller to reduce divinity to human and animal stature—a desire which is entirely in accordance with the world view of the magician. Santayana, we can see, has put it rightly when he observes that "the first function of mythology is to justify magic."

The system of taboo also has its influence on myth. Taboo, which may be described as "negative magic," is a social and psychological device for preserving the separation between the matter-of-fact world and the preternatural world. An object or a being which has *mana* is regarded as dangerous if it is not treated with the proper magical technique and so it is set apart—"insulated," as Marett says—from the ordinary world and its techniques. A number of myths dramatize this isolation of the preternatural by reasserting its importance: myths which tell of the breaking of a taboo—such as those of Orpheus and Eurydice, Cupid and Psyche, or Lot's wife—are examples.

The question of the relation between myth and religion is a difficult one. If the reader has sometimes gained the impression that this book is a study of religion as much as of myth, that is partly due to the bias of the available literature. The missionaries who first wrote about primitive society were naturally interested primarily in religion, and so were the philosophers who studied their reports. Even the books by modern anthropologists which we have consulted for information about myth have been in many cases treatises on religion rather than on myth. This all gives the impression that religion and myth in primitive society amount to about the same thing. There is no doubt, however, that a great many myths are clearly extraneous to religion. These may be political or economic myths—stories of genealogy and social tradition which lend credence or support to a political caste or an economic system. Or they may be—like some of the cosmological and cosmogonic myths of the Polynesians—creations of philosophically-minded individuals whose imagination liberates itself from the system of ritual and ceremony which for their fellows is inviolable and which constitutes the religion of the society. Some students of myth, such as Hume and Lang, say that there is a deep-seated enmity between myth and religion and that the great body of popular mythology is antireligious. If we define religion as moral theism, this is undoubtedly true. The idea that there is an enmity between myth and religion contains a large element of truth, as we shall see, even if, with Tylor, we define religion as "the belief in spiritual beings." If, on the other hand, we mean by religion the whole magico-religious complex, then we may say that the great majority of myths are religion in literary form. We should not, however, confuse religion with theology. Theology and theological dogma have always been the preoccupation of a very limited number of men; and a purely theological myth is an impossibility.

The influence of exceptional individuals upon myth has come to seem more and more important in recent decades; and a full study of these individuals and their relations with the mass of men would doubtless help us to find our way about in the bewildering variety of mythology. We can at least glance at this question briefly. Professor Boas writes that "the parallelism of

140

distribution of religious or social groups led by single individuals and of complex mythologies is so striking that there can be little doubt in regard to their psychological connection. The Mexicans, the Pueblo tribes, the Pawnee, the Bella Coola, the Maidu may be given as examples. The contrast between a disorganized mass of folktales and the more systematic mythologies seems to lie, therefore, in the introduction of an element of *individual* creativeness in the latter. The priest or chief as a poet or thinker takes hold of the folk traditions and of isolated rituals and elaborates them in dramatic or poetic form. Their systematization is brought about by the centralization of thought in one mind." Here again we are at the mercy of the available literature. The individuals whom anthropologists have studied are primarily religious leaders, and we cannot say definitely to what extent the religious leader is the creator of myths, or to what extent the creator of myths is religious. Important questions such as the temperament and social position and function of the primitive literary man (in so far as he is identifiable as such) must go unanswered until a study is made of him. Like the poets and critics of the late eighteenth century we would like to know more about the primitive bard. The religious leader, however, must have exerted a powerful influence either directly or indirectly on the making of myths; and we do know something of him.

According to Paul Radin, the religious leader is motivated by two complementary desires: to consolidate his position as a member of an economically privileged caste and to satisfy his craving as an intellectual for order, objectivity, and form. His task is "to interpret and manipulate the psychological correlates of the economic-social realities." The priest-thinker is of course generally in favor of religion rather than magic, and his lifework is devoted to displacing or reinterpreting magic—in other words, to divesting the individual of the prerogative he gains from magic and to transferring power from man to the gods. Thus his pur-

141

pose is to establish a belief in spiritual beings who have objective reality and exist independently of magical practices; for, to the ordinary man, spirits and gods, if they exist at all, seem to do so only when they produce desired effects, and even then they are far from clearly conceived. The priest's task is to transfer the emotions attached to magic technique and belief to religion. To this end he creates independent, powerful gods, and, as Radin says, establishes a variety of spirits and deities who retain many of the qualities of the magical imagination and who are still close to the "life-values" of man. These spirits and deities, a kind of compromise between magic and religion, are the stock in trade of mythmakers; the tensions aroused and the reconciliations effected between the religious desire for an omnipotent deity and the general human preference for powerful anthropomorphic and theriomorphic beings are universally stamped upon mythology. We feel something of this tension, for example, in the wars of the Titans against God or, as in Grimm's *Fairy Tales,* the battle of man and his friendly animals against the devilish monsters. Radin has found traces of the different stages of this struggle in Winnebago myth. In one myth the young buffalo spirits in heaven are warned not to smell the smoke of tobacco offerings rising from the earth because if they do they will be doomed to descend to earth as real buffaloes and be shot. Here the magical prerogative remains; the spirits are partly in the power of man. Other myths place man in a more abject position. Thus Earthmaker, the supreme, or at least superior, god of the Winnebagos is said to have given all of his gifts to the spirits (just as Epimetheus gives all of *his* to the animals) so that he had none left for man, whom he created last. Therefore he condescends to grant the requests of man if they are correctly made. In myths which are still more religious the spirits are openly contemptuous of man and plague him by sending spurious messengers to suppliants, or man is portrayed in complete abjection before the gods.

Psychologically we may state the difference between magic and religion thus: magic is the envelopment and coercion of the objective world by the ego; it is a dynamic subjectivism. Religion is the coercion of the ego by gods and spirits who are objectively conceived beings in control of nature and man. This fundamental clash of emotions and attitudes must be felt pervasively, if unconsciously, in primitive society (the terms we have used could probably be translated so as to apply to civilized society as well as primitive). I suggest that myth dramatizes in poetic form the disharmonies, the deep neurotic disturbances which may be occasioned by this clash of inward and outward forces, and that by reconciling the opposing forces, by making them interact coercively toward a common end, myth performs a profoundly beneficial and life-giving act. This I call the Promethean function of myth. For Prometheus is the intermediary between God and man. He is the dynamic principle and art of life, and he helps man to defend himself against the old Zeus, who treacherously seeks, as Toynbee writes, to set "his foot on the neck of a prostrate Universe." It is the destiny of Zeus to grow remote, tyrannical, frozen, inhuman, and reactionary. It is the destiny of man to rebel against this tyranny. Prometheus resolves the struggle in favor of man and shows him how to use the energies called forth by his war against Zeus.

9

The Archetypes of Literature

BY NORTHROP FRYE

Every organized body of knowledge can be learned progressively; and experience shows that there is also something progressive about the learning of literature. Our opening sentence has already got us into a semantic difficulty. Physics is an organized body of knowledge about nature, and a student of it says that he is learning physics, not that he is learning nature. Art, like nature, is the subject of a systematic study, and has to be distinguished from the study itself, which is criticism. It is therefore impossible to "learn literature": one learns about it in a certain way, but what one learns, transitively, is the criticism of literature. Similarly, the difficulty often felt in "teaching literature" arises from the fact that it cannot be done: the criticism of literature is all that can be directly taught. So while no one expects literature itself to behave like a science, there is surely no reason why criticism, as a systematic and organized study, should not be, at least partly, a science. Not a "pure" or "exact" science, perhaps, but these phrases form part of a 19th Century cosmology which is no longer with us. Criticism deals with the arts and may well be something of an art itself, but it does not follow that it must be unsystematic. If it is to be related to the sciences too, it does not follow that it must be deprived of the graces of culture.

Certainly criticism as we find it in learned journals and scholarly monographs has every characteristic of a science. Evidence is examined scientifically; previous authorities are used scientifically; fields are investigated scientifically; texts are edited scientifically. Prosody is scientific in structure; so is phonetics; so is philology. And yet in studying this kind of critical science the student becomes aware of a centrifugal movement carrying him away from literature. He finds that literature is the central division of the "humanities," flanked on one side by history and on the other by philosophy. Criticism so far ranks only as a subdivision of literature; and hence, for the systematic mental organization of the subject, the student has to turn to the conceptual framework of the historian for events, and to that of the philosopher for ideas. Even the more centrally placed critical sciences, such as textual editing, seem to be part of a "background" that recedes into history or some other non-literary field. The thought suggests itself that the ancillary critical disciplines may be related to a central expanding pattern of systematic comprehension which has not yet been established, but which, if it were established, would prevent them from being centrifugal. If such a pattern exists, then criticism would be to art what philosophy is to wisdom and history to action.

Most of the central area of criticism is at present, and doubtless always will be, the area of commentary. But the commentators have little sense, unlike the researchers, of being contained within some sort of scientific discipline: they are chiefly engaged, in the words of the gospel hymn, in brightening the corner where they are. If we attempt to get a more comprehensive idea of what criticism is about, we find ourselves wandering over quaking bogs of generalities, judicious pronouncements of value, reflective comments, perorations to works of research, and other consequences of taking the large view. But this part of the critical field is so full of pseudo-propositions, sonorous nonsense that contains no truth and no falsehood, that it obviously exists only because criticism, like nature, prefers a waste space to an empty one.

The term "pseudo-proposition" may imply some sort of logical positivist attitude on my own part. But I would not confuse the significant proposition with the factual one; nor should I consider it advisable to muddle the study of literature with a schizophrenic dichotomy between subjective-emotional and objective-descriptive aspects of meaning, considering that in order to produce any literary meaning at all one has to ignore this dichotomy. I say only that the principles by which one can distinguish a significant from a meaningless statement in criticism are not clearly defined. Our first step, therefore, is to recognize and get rid of meaningless criticism: that is, talking about literature in a way that cannot help to build up a systematic structure of knowledge. Casual value-judgments belong not to criticism but to the history of taste, and reflect, at best, only the social and psychological compulsions which prompted their utterance. All judgments in which the values are not based on literary experience but are sentimental or derived from religious or political prejudice may be regarded as casual. Sentimental judgments are usually based either on nonexistent categories or antitheses ("Shakespeare studied life, Milton books") or on a visceral reaction to the writer's personality. The literary chit-chat which makes the reputations of poets boom and crash in an imaginary stock exchange is pseudo-criticism. That wealthy investor Mr. Eliot, after dumping Milton on the market, is now buying him again; Donne has probably reached his peak and will begin to taper off; Tennyson may be in for a slight flutter but the Shelley stocks are still bearish. This sort of thing cannot be part of any systematic study, for a systematic study can only progress: whatever dithers or vacillates or reacts is merely leisure-class conversation.

We next meet a more serious group of critics who say: the foreground of criticism is the impact of literature on the reader. Let us, then, keep the study of literature centripetal, and base the learning process on a structural analysis of the literary work itself. The texture of any great work of art is complex and ambiguous, and in unravelling the complexities we may take in as much history and philosophy as we please, if the subject of our study remains at the center. If it does not, we may find that in our anxiety to write about literature we have forgotten how to read it.

The only weakness in this approach is that it is conceived primarily as the antithesis of centrifugal or "background" criticism, and so lands us in a somewhat unreal dilemma, like the conflict of internal and external relations in philosophy. Antitheses are usually resolved, not by picking one side and refuting the other, or by making eclectic choices between them, but by trying to get past the antithetical way of stating the problem. It is right that the first effort of critical apprehension should take the form of a rhetorical or structural analysis of a work of art. But a purely structural approach has the same limitation in criticism that it has in biology. In itself it is simply a discrete series of analyses based on the mere existence of the literary structure, without developing any explanation of how the structure came to be what it was and what its nearest relatives are. Structural analysis brings rhetoric back to criticism, but we need a new poetics as well, and the attempt to construct a new poetics out of rhetoric alone can hardly avoid a mere complication of rhetorical terms into a sterile jargon. I suggest that what is at present missing from literary criticism is a co-ordinating principle, a central hypothesis which, like the theory of evolution in biology, will see the phenomena it deals with as parts of a whole. Such a principle, though it would retain the centripetal perspective of structural analysis, would try to give the same perspective to other kinds of criticism too.

The first postulate of this hypothesis is the same as that of any science: the assumption of total coherence. The assumption refers to the science, not to what it deals with. A belief in an order of nature is an inference from the intelligibility of the natural sciences; and if the natural sciences ever completely demonstrated the order of nature they would presumably exhaust their subject. Criticism, as a science, is totally intelligible; literature, as the subject of a science, is, so far as we know, an inexhaustible source of new critical discoveries, and would be even if new works of literature ceased to be written. If so, then the search for a limiting principle in literature in order to discourage the development of criticism is mistaken. The assertion that the critic should not look for more in a poem than the poet may safely be assumed to have been conscious of putting there is a common form of what may be called the fallacy of premature teleology. It corresponds to the assertion that a natural phenomenon is as it is because Providence in its inscutable wisdom made it so.

Simple as the assumption appears, it takes a long time for a science to discover that it is in fact a totally intelligible body of knowledge. Until it makes this discovery it has not been born as an individual science, but remains an embryo within the body of some other subject. The birth of physics from "natural philosophy" and of sociology from "moral philosophy" will illustrate the process. It is also very approximately true that the modern sciences have developed in the order of their closeness to mathematics. Thus physics and astronomy assumed their modern form in the Renaissance, chemistry in the 18th Century, biology in the 19th, and the social sciences in the 20th. If systematic criticism, then, is developing only in our day, the fact is at least not an anachronism.

We are now looking for classifying principles lying in an area between two points that we have fixed. The first of these is the preliminary effort of criticism, the structural analysis of the work of art. The second is the assumption that there is such a subject as criticism, and that it makes, or could make, complete sense. We may next proceed inductively from structural analysis, associating the data we collect and trying to see larger patterns in them. Or we may proceed deductively, with the consequences that follow from postulating the unity of criticism. It is clear, of course, that neither procedure will work indefinitely without correction from the other. Pure induction will get us lost in haphazard guessing; pure deduction will lead to inflexible and over-simplified pigeon-holing. Let us now attempt a few tentative steps in each direction, beginning with the inductive one.

II

The unity of a work of art, the basis of structural analysis, has not been produced solely by the unconditioned will of the artist, for the artist is only its efficient cause: it has form, and consequently a formal cause. The fact that revision is possible, that the poet makes changes not because he likes them better but because they are better, means that poems, like poets, are born and not made. The poet's task is to deliver the poem in as uninjured a state as possible, and if the poem is alive, it is equally anxious to be rid of him, and screams to be cut loose from his private memories and associations, his desire for self-expression, and all other navel-strings and feeding tubes of his ego. The critic takes over where the poet leaves off, and criticism can hardly do without a kind of literary psychology connecting the poet with the poem. Part of this may be a psychological study of the poet, though this is useful chiefly in analysing the failures in his expression, the things in him which are still attached to his work. More important is the fact that every poet has his private mythology, his own spectroscopic band or peculiar formation of symbols, of much of which he is quite unconscious. In works with characters of their own, such as dramas and novels, the same psychological analysis may be extended to the interplay of characters, though of course literary psychology would analyse the behavior of such characters only in relation to literary convention.

There is still before us the problem of the formal cause of

the poem, a problem deeply involved with the question of genres. We cannot say much about genres, for criticism does not know much about them. A good many critical efforts to grapple with such words as "novel" or "epic" are chiefly interesting as examples of the psychology of rumor. Two conceptions of the genre, however, are obviously fallacious, and as they are opposite extremes, the truth must lie somewhere between them. One is the pseudo-Platonic conception of genres as existing prior to and independently of creation, which confuses them with mere conventions of form like the sonnet. The other is that pseudo-biological conception of them as evolving species which turns up in so many surveys of the "development" of this or that form.

We next inquire for the origin of the genre, and turn first of all to the social conditions and cultural demands which produced it—in other words to the material cause of the work of art. This leads us into literary history, which differs from ordinary history in that its containing categories, "Gothic," "Baroque," "Romantic," and the like are cultural categories, of little use to the ordinary historian. Most literary history does not get as far as these categories, but even so we know more about it than about most kinds of critical scholarship. The historian treats literature and philosophy historically; the philosopher treats history and literature philosophically; and the so-called "history of ideas" approach marks the beginning of an attempt to treat history and philosophy from the point of view of an autonomous criticism.

But still we feel that there is something missing. We say that every poet has his own peculiar formation of images. But when so many poets use so many of the same images, surely there are much bigger critical problems involved than biographical ones. As Mr. Auden's brilliant essay *The Enchafèd Flood* shows, an important symbol like the sea cannot remain within the poetry of Shelley or Keats or Coleridge: it is bound to expand over many poets into an archetypal symbol of literature. And if the genre has a historical origin, why does the genre of drama emerge from medieval religion in a way so strikingly similar to the way it emerged from Greek religion centuries before? This is a problem of structure rather than origin, and suggests that there may be archetypes of genres as well as of images.

It is clear that criticism cannot be systematic unless there is a quality in literature which enables it to be so, an order of words corresponding to the order of nature in the natural sciences. An archetype should be not only a unifying category of criticism, but itself a part of a total form, and it leads us at once to the question of what sort of total form criticism can see in literature. Our survey of critical techniques has taken us as far as literary history. Total literary history moves from the primitive to the sophisticated, and here we glimpse the possibility of seeing literature as a complication of a relatively restricted and simple group of formulas that can be studied in primitive culture. If so, then the search for archetypes is a kind of literary anthropology, concerned with the way that literature is informed by preliterary categories such as ritual, myth and folk tale. We next realize that the relation between these categories and literature is by no means purely one of descent, as we find them reappearing in the greatest classics—in fact there seems to be a general tendency on the part of great classics to revert to them. This coincides with a feeling that we have all had: that the study of mediocre works of art, however energetic, obstinately remains a random and peripheral form of critical experience, whereas the profound masterpiece seems to draw us to a point at which we can see an enormous number of converging patterns of significance. Here we begin to wonder if we cannot see literature, not only as complicating itself in time, but as spread out in conceptual space from some unseen center.

This inductive movement towards the archetype is a process

of backing up, as it were, from structural analysis, as we back up from a painting if we want to see composition instead of brushwork. In the foreground of the grave-digger scene in *Hamlet,* for instance, is an intricate verbal texture, ranging from the puns of the first clown to the *danse macabre* of the Yorick soliloquy, which we study in the printed text. One step back, and we are in the Wilson Knight and Spurgeon group of critics, listening to the steady rain of images of corruption and decay. Here too, as the sense of the place of this scene in the whole play begins to dawn on us, we are in the network of psychological relationships which were the main interest of Bradley. But after all, we say, we are forgetting the genre: *Hamlet* is a play, and an Elizabethan play. So we take another step back into the Stoll and Shaw group and see the scene conventionally as part of its dramatic context. One step more, and we can begin to glimpse the archetype of the scene, as the hero's *Liebestod* and first unequivocal declaration of his love, his struggle with Laertes and the sealing of his own fate, and the sudden sobering of his mood that marks the transition to the final scene, all take shape around a leap into and return from the grave that has so weirdly yawned open on the stage.

At each stage of understanding this scene we are dependent on a certain kind of scholarly organization. We need first an editor to clean up the text for us, then the rhetorician and philologist, then the literary psychologist. We cannot study the genre without the help of the literary social historian, the literary philosopher and the student of the "history of ideas," and for the archetype we need a literary anthropologist. But now that we have got our central pattern of criticism established, all these interests are seen as converging on literary criticism instead of receding from it into psychology and history and the rest. In particular, the literary anthropologist who chases the source of the Hamlet legend from the pre-Shakespeare play to Saxo, and from Saxo to nature-myths, is not running away from Shakespeare: he is drawing closer to the archetypal form which Shakespeare recreated. A minor result of our new perspective is that contradictions among critics, and assertions that this and not that critical approach is the right one, show a remarkable tendency to dissolve into unreality. Let us now see what we can get from the deductive end.

III

Some arts move in time, like music; others are presented in space, like painting. In both cases the organizing principle is recurrence, which is called rhythm when it is temporal and pattern when it is spatial. Thus we speak of the rhythm of music and the pattern of painting; but later, to show off our sophistication, we may begin to speak of the rhythm of painting and the pattern of music. In other words, all arts may be conceived both temporally and spatially. The score of a musical composition may be studied all at once; a picture may be seen as the track of an intricate dance of the eye. Literature seems to be intermediate between music and painting: its words form rhythms which approach a musical sequence of sounds at one of its boundaries, and form patterns which approach the hieroglyphic or pictorial image at the other. The attempts to get as near to these boundaries as possible form the main body of what is called experimental writing. We may call the rhythm of literature the narrative, and the pattern, the simultaneous mental grasp of the verbal structure, the meaning or significance. We hear or listen to a narrative, but when we grasp a writer's total pattern we "see" what he means.

The criticism of literature is much more hampered by the representational fallacy than even the criticism of painting. That is why we are apt to think of narrative as a sequential representation of events in an outside "life," and of meaning as a reflection of some external "idea." Properly used as critical terms, an author's narrative is his linear movement; his meaning is the integrity of his completed form. Similarly an image is not merely a verbal replica of an external object, but any unit of a verbal structure seen as part of a total pattern or rhythm. Even the letters an author spells his words with form part of his imagery, though only in special cases (such as alliteration) would they call for critical notice. Narrative and meaning thus become respectively, to borrow musical terms, the melodic and harmonic contexts of the imagery.

Rhythm, or recurrent movement, is deeply founded on the natural cycle, and everything in nature that we think of as having some analogy with works of art, like the flower or the bird's song, grows out of a profound synchronization between an organism and the rhythms of its environment, especially that of the solar year. With animals some expressions of synchronization, like the mating dances of birds, could almost be called rituals. But in human life a ritual seems to be something of a voluntary effort (hence the magical element in it) to recapture a lost rapport with the natural cycle. A farmer must harvest his crop at a certain time of year, but because this is involuntary, harvesting itself is not precisely a ritual. It is the deliberate expression of a will to synchronize human and natural energies at that time which produces the harvest songs, harvest sacrifices and harvest folk customs that we call rituals. In ritual, then, we may find the origin of narrative, a ritual being a temporal sequence of acts in which the conscious meaning or significance is latent: it can be seen by an observer, but is largely concealed from the participators themselves. The pull of ritual is toward pure narrative, which, if there could be such a thing, would be automatic and unconscious repetition. We should notice too the regular tendency of ritual to become encyclopedic. All the important recurrences in nature, the day, the phases of the moon, the seasons and solstices of the year, the crises of existence from birth to death, get rituals attached to them, and most of the higher religions are equipped with a definitive total body of rituals suggestive, if we may put it so, of the entire range of potentially significant actions in human life.

Patterns of imagery, on the other hand, or fragments of significance, are oracular in origin, and derive from the epiphanic moment, the flash of instantaneous comprehension with no direct reference to time, the importance of which is indicated by Cassirer in *Myth and Language*. By the time we get them, in the form of proverbs, riddles, commandments and etiological folk tales, there is already a considerable element of narrative in them. They too are encyclopedic in tendency, building up a total structure of significance, or doctrine, from random and empiric fragments. And just as pure narrative would be unconscious act, so pure significance would be an incommunicable state of consciousness, for communication begins by constructing narrative.

The myth is the central informing power that gives archetypal significance to the ritual and archetypal narrative to the oracle. Hence the myth *is* the archetype, though it might be convenient to say myth only when referring to narrative, and archetype when speaking of significance. In the solar cycle of the day, the seasonal cycle of the year, and the organic cycle of human life, there is a single pattern of significance, out of which myth constructs a central narrative around a figure who is partly the sun, partly vegetative fertility and partly a god or archetypal human being. The crucial importance of this myth has been forced on literary critics by Jung and Frazer in particular, but the several books now available on it are not always systematic in their approach, for which reason I supply the following table of its phases:

1.

The dawn, spring and birth phase. Myths of the birth of

the hero, of revival and resurrection, of creation and (because the four phases are a cycle) of the defeat of the powers of darkness, winter and death. Subordinate characters: the father and the mother. The archetype of romance and of most dithyrambic and rhapsodic poetry.

2.

The zenith, summer, and marriage or triumph phase. Myths of apotheosis, of the sacred marriage, and of entering into Paradise. Subordinate characters: the companion and the bride. The archetype of comedy, pastoral and idyll.

3.

The sunset, autumn and death phase. Myths of fall, of the dying god, of violent death and sacrifice and of the isolation of the hero. Subordinate characters: the traitor and the siren. The archetype of tragedy and elegy.

4.

The darkness, winter and dissolution phase. Myths of the triumph of these powers; myths of floods and the return of chaos, of the defeat of the hero, and Götterdämmerung myths. Subordinate characters: the ogre and the witch. The archetype of satire (see, for instance, the conclusion of *The Dunciad*).

The quest of the hero also tends to assimilate the oracular and random verbal structures, as we can see when we watch the chaos of local legends that results from prophetic epiphanies consolidating into a narrative mythology of departmental gods. In most of the higher religions this in turn has become the same central quest-myth that emerges from ritual, as the Messiah myth became the narrative structure of the oracles of Judaism. A local flood may beget a folk tale by accident, but a comparison of flood stories will show how quickly such tales became examples of the myth of dissolution. Finally, the tendency of both ritual and epiphany to become encyclopedic is realized in the definitive body of myth which constitutes the sacred scriptures of religions. These sacred scriptures are consequently the first documents that the literary critic has to study to gain a comprehensive view of his subject. After he has understood their structure, then he can descend from archetypes to genres, and see how the drama emerges from the ritual side of myth and lyric from the epiphanic or fragmented side, while the epic carries on the central encyclopedic structure.

Some words of caution and encouragement are necessary before literary criticism has clearly staked out its boundaries in these fields. It is part of the critic's business to show how all literary genres are derived from the quest-myth, but the derivation is a logical one within the science of criticism: the quest-myth will constitute the first chapter of whatever future handbooks of criticism may be written that will be based on enough organized critical knowledge to call themselves "introductions" or "outlines" and still be able to live up to their titles. It is only when we try to expound the derivation chronologically that we find ourselves writing pseudo-prehistorical fictions and theories of mythological contract. Again, because psychology and anthropology are more highly developed sciences, the critic who deals with this kind of material is bound to appear, for some time, a dilettante of those subjects. These two phases of criticism are largely undeveloped in comparison with literary history and rhetoric, the reason being the later development of the sciences they are related to. But the fascination which *The Golden Bough* and Jung's book on libido symbols have for literary critics is not based on dilettantism, but on the fact that these books are primarily studies in literary criticism, and very important ones.

In any case the critic who is studying the principles of literary form has a quite different interest from the psychologist's concern with states of mind or the anthropologist's with social institutions. For instance: the mental response to narrative is mainly passive; to significance mainly active. From this fact Ruth Benedict's *Patterns of Culture* develops a distinction between "Apollonian" cultures based on obedience to ritual and "Dionysiac" ones based on a tense exposure of the prophetic mind to epiphany. The critic would tend rather to note how popular literature which appeals to the inertia of the untrained mind puts a heavy emphasis on narrative values, whereas a sophisticated atttempt to disrupt the connection between the poet and his environment produces the Rimbaud type of *illumination*, Joyce's solitary epiphanies, and Baudelaire's conception of nature as a source of oracles. Also how literature, as it develops from the primitive to the self-conscious, shows a gradual shift of the poet's attention from narrative to significant values, this shift of attention being the basis of Schiller's distinction between naive and sentimental poetry.

The relation of criticism to religion, when they deal with the same documents, is more complicated. In criticism, as in history, the divine is always treated as a human artifact. God for the critic, whether he finds him in *Paradise Lost* or the Bible, is a character in a human story; and for the critic all epiphanies are explained, not in terms of the riddle of a possessing god or devil, but as mental phenomena closely associated in their origin with dreams. This once established, it is then necessary to say that nothing in criticism or art compels the critic to take the attitude of ordinary waking consciousness towards the dream or the god. Art deals not with the real but with the conceivable; and criticism, though it will eventually have to have some theory of conceivability, can never be justified in trying to develop, much less assume, any theory of actuality. It is necessary to understand this before our next and final point can be made.

We have identified the central myth of literature, in its narrative aspect, with the quest-myth. Now if we wish to see this central myth as a pattern of meaning also, we have to start with the workings of the subconscious where the epiphany originates, in other words in the dream. The human cycle of waking and dreaming corresponds closely to the natural cycle of light and darkness, and it is perhaps in this correspondence that all imaginative life begins. The correspondence is largely an antithesis: it is in daylight that man is really in the power of darkness, a prey to frustration and weakness; it is in the darkness of nature that the "libido" or conquering heroic self awakes. Hence art, which Plato called a dream for awakened minds, seems to have as its final cause the resolution of the antithesis, the mingling of the sun and the hero, the realizing of a world in which the inner desire and the outward circumstance coincide. This is the same goal, of course, that the attempt to combine human and natural power in ritual has. The social function of the arts, therefore, seems to be closely connected with visualizing the goal of work in human life. So in terms of significance, the central myth of art must be the vision of the end of social effort, the innocent world of fulfilled desires, the free human society. Once this is understood, the integral place of criticism among the other social sciences, in interpreting and systematizing the vision of the artist, will be easier to see. It is at this point that we can see how religious conceptions of the final cause of human effort are as relevant as any others to criticism.

The importance of the god or hero in the myth lies in the fact that such characters, who are conceived in human likeness and yet have more power over nature, gradually build up the vision of an omnipotent personal community beyond an indifferent nature. It is this community which the hero regularly enters in his apotheosis. The world of this apotheosis thus begins to pull away from the rotary cycle of the quest in which all triumph is temporary. Hence if we look at the quest-myth as a pattern of imagery, we see the hero's quest first of all in terms of its fulfilment. This gives us our central pattern of archetypal images, the vision of innocence which sees the world in terms of total human intelligibility. It corresponds to, and is usually found in the form of, the vision of the unfallen world or heaven in religion. We may call it the comic vision of life, in contrast to the tragic vision, which sees the quest only in the form of its ordained cycle.

We conclude with a second table of contents, in which we shall attempt to set forth the central pattern of the comic and tragic visions. One essential principle of archetypal criticism is that the individual and the universal forms of an image are identical, the reasons being too complicated for us just now. We proceed according to the general plan of the game of Twenty Questions, or, if we prefer, of the Great Chain of Being:

1.

In the comic vision the *human* world is a community, or a hero who represents the wish-fulfillment of the reader. The archetype of images of symposium, communion, order, friendship and love. In the tragic vision the human world is a tyranny or anarchy, or an individual or isolated man, the leader with his back to his followers, the bullying giant of romance, the deserted or betrayed hero. Marriage or some equivalent consummation belongs to the comic vision; the harlot, witch and other varieties of Jung's "terrible mother" belong to the tragic one. All divine, heroic, angelic or other superhuman communities follow the human pattern.

2.

In the comic vision the *animal* world is a community of domesticated animals, usually a flock of sheep, or a lamb, or one of the gentler birds, usually a dove. The archetype of pastoral images. In the tragic vision the animal world is seen in terms of beasts and birds of prey, wolves, vultures, serpents, dragons and the like.

3.

In the comic vision the *vegetable* world is a garden, grove or park, or a tree of life, or a rose or lotus. The archetype of Arcadian images, such as that of Marvell's green world or of Shakespeare's forest comedies. In the tragic vision it is a sinister forest like the one in *Comus* or at the opening of the *Inferno*, or a heath or wilderness, or a tree of death.

4.

In the comic vision the *mineral* world is a city, or one building or temple, or one stone, normally a glowing precious stone— in fact the whole comic series, especially the tree, can be conceived as luminous or fiery. The archetype of geometrical images: the "starlit dome" belongs here. In the tragic vision the mineral world is seen in terms of deserts, rocks and ruins, or of sinister geometrical images like the cross.

5.

In the comic vision the *unformed* world is a river, traditionally fourfold, which influenced the Renaissance image of the temperate body with its four humors. In the tragic vision this world usually becomes the sea, as the narrative myth of dissolution is so often a flood myth. The combination of the sea and beast images gives us the leviathan and similar water-monsters.

Obvious as this table looks, a great variety of poetic images and forms will be found to fit it. Yeats's "Sailing to Byzantium," to take a famous example of the comic vision at random, has the city, the tree, the bird, the community of sages, the geometrical gyre and the detachment from the cyclic world. It is, of course, only the general comic or tragic context that determines the interpretation of any symbol: this is obvious with relatively neutral archetypes like the island, which may be Prospero's island or Circe's.

Our tables are, of course, not only elementary but grossly over-simplified, just as our inductive approach to the archetype was a mere hunch. The important point is not the deficiencies of either procedure, taken by itself, but the fact that, somewhere and somehow, the two are clearly going to meet in the middle. And if they do meet, the ground plan of a systematic and comprehensive development of criticism has been established.

Selected Bibliography

1. *General works*: The best large collection of fictional criticism is *Critiques and Essays on Modern Fiction, 1920-1951*, ed. by John W. Aldridge (New York: The Ronald Press Company, 1952). Its lengthy bibliography, compiled by Robert Wooster Stallman, is especially valuable. Another important collection is *Forms of Modern Fiction*, ed. by William Van O'Connor (Minneapolis: The University of Minnesota Press, 1948).

2. *Artists and Theories*: The serious student of fiction should become acquainted with Henry James' Prefaces to his New York edition which have been collected as *The Art of the Novel* (New York: Charles Scribner's Sons, 1947). Two valuable collections of the commentary of artists are: *Novelists on the Novel*, ed. by Miriam Allott (New York: Columbia University Press, 1959), and *Writers on Writing*, ed. by Walter Allen (Boston: The Writer, 1959).

3. *Craft and Technique*: The classic is, of course, Percy Lubbock's *The Craft of Fiction* (New York: Peter Smith, 1945). Important volumes on this subject include Robert Humphrey's *Stream of Consciousness in the Modern Novel* (Berkeley: University of California Press, 1954); Melvin J. Friedman's *Stream of Consciousness: A Study in Literary Method* (New Haven: Yale University Press, 1955), which includes a good bibliography; and Leon Edel, *The Psychological Novel, 1900-1950* (New York: J. B. Lippincott Company, 1955).

4. *Openings and Extensions*: The reader should look first at all of E. M. Forster's *Aspects of the Novel* (New York: Harcourt Brace, 1927). Among additional important volumes are: Edmund Wilson, *Axel's Castle* (New York: Charles Scribner's Sons, 1948); Richard Chase, *Quest for Myth* (Baton Rouge: Louisiana State University Press, 1949); William York Tindall, *The Literary Symbol* (New York: Columbia University Press, 1955); and Northrop Frye, *Anatomy of Criticism* (Princeton: Princeton University Press, 1957).

A NOTE ABOUT THE EDITOR

James E. Miller, Jr. has been Professor of English and Chairman of the Department at the University of Nebraska since 1956. Born in 1920, he took his A.B. degree at the University of Oklahoma (1942) and his M.A. and Ph.D. at the University of Chicago (1947, 1949). After a year as an instructor at the University of Michigan, he went to Nebraska as an assistant professor in 1953. He served in the Army during World War II from 1942 to 1946 and in the Korean War, 1950-1952. Awarded a Fulbright lectureship in 1958-1959, he lectured at the Oriental Institute in Naples and at the University of Rome. In 1960 he was appointed Editor of *College English* by the National Council of Teachers of English.

Dr. Miller has contributed some thirty articles, sketches, stories, and reviews to scholarly and literary periodicals. He is the author of *A Critical Guide to Leaves of Grass* (1957), which won the Walt Whitman Award of the Poetry Society of America, and *The Fictional Technique of Scott Fitzgerald* (1957); editor of *Walt Whitman: Complete Poetry and Selected Poems* (1959); and co-author, with Karl Shapiro and Bernice Slote, of START WITH THE SUN: STUDIES IN COSMIC POETRY (1960), published by the University of Nebraska Press.